TEACHINGS
FROM THE
LONGHOUSE

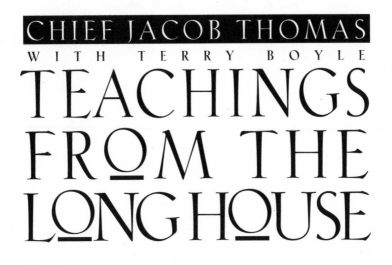

CHIEF JACOB THOMAS

WITH TERRY BOYLE

TEACHINGS FROM THE LONG HOUSE

Stoddart

First published in 1994 by
Stoddart Publishing Co. Limited
34 Lesmill Road
Toronto, Canada
M3B 2T6
(416) 445-3333

Second printing May 1995

Canadian Cataloguing in Publication Data

Thomas, Jacob E.
Teachings from the longhouse

ISBN 0-7737-2745-0

1. Indians of North America — Religion and mythology.
I. Boyle, Terry.   II. Title.

E98.R3T56 1994   299'.7   C94-930037-3

Typesetting: Tony Gordon Ltd.

Printed and bound in Canada

*Stoddart Publishing gratefully acknowledges the support of the Canada Council, Ontario
Ministry of Culture, Tourism, and Recreation, Ontario Arts Council, and Ontario
Publishing Centre in the development of writing and publishing in Canada.*

Contents

TEACHINGS FROM THE LONG HOUSE

Introduction

LATE ONE DAY last year I received a phone call that would alter my life and my way of thinking. The caller was Chief Jacob Thomas, hereditary chief of the Six Nations. Jake, as he likes to be called, and I had never met. He was calling to ask if we could meet and discuss something that was on his mind. A week later he knocked at the back door and entered our home and our hearts. Chief Jacob Thomas had come to ask me to work with him on writing his *Teachings from the Longhouse*. We began our journey together discussing the meaning of this book with a few others in our home.

Teachings from the Longhouse outlines the Code of Handsome Lake, the precepts of a North American religion that is still practised on Iroquois reservations in the United States and Canada. It is essentially an amalgam of ancient tradition and the revelations of the Seneca prophet Handsome Lake. The heart of the Handsome Lake religion is the Good Word or Good Message (the *Gaiwí:yo*) — a teaching transmitted by word of mouth from faithkeeper to faithkeeper. Each faithkeeper memorizes the Good Message and chants it before the people in the Longhouse twice a year, hour after hour, for the mornings of four days.

The Code itself is many things: a narrative of the vision of Handsome Lake and his travels as a bringer of the Good Message, a catalogue of sins and their punishments, a description of heaven and hell, a definition of the good way of life, a prescription for the proper ceremonies to be performed in the Longhouse. Drinking, witchcraft, theft, quarrelsomeness, gossip, wife beating, adultery, abortion, jealousy — these things are all dealt with in the Code. Husbands and wives are to love one another; children are to be treated with kindness; humans must be reverent to the Great Spirit and His creation. Like the Christian's Bible, the Code of Handsome Lake combines history and prophecy, commandment and exhortation, and above all, provides an order of conduct by which men and women may live honourably in this world and happily in the next.

The world in which Handsome Lake grew to manhood, and in which he took his place as an active hunter and warrior, was the world of an unvanquished Iroquois nation. The Seneca were the most populous and powerful of the confederated Iroquois tribes. They numbered about four thousand people, and their tribal territory extended from the upper waters of the Allegheny and Susquehanna rivers on the south, to Lake Ontario on the north. The western marches of the Seneca territory were the shores of Lake Erie. To the east, beyond Seneca Lake, were the Cayuga people. The other Iroquoian tribes — Onondaga, Oneida, Tuscarora, and Mohawk — lay successively eastward almost to the Hudson River.

The entire area occupied by the Iroquois Confederacy

between the Hudson River and Lake Erie was likened by the Iroquois themselves to a longhouse compartmented by tribes. In this "longhouse" the Seneca were "the keepers of the western door." They were the guardians of the portal from which the Iroquois warriors traditionally departed to attack the western and southern nations, the portal through which Iroquois hunters passed to exploit the conquered lands along the Allegheny and Ohio, and the portal where other nations had to build a fire and await an invitation brought by a runner before entering the country of the Confederacy. The Iroquois travelled from Hudson Bay to the mountains of the Carolinas, and from the Atlantic to the Mississippi, to fight members of alien tribes and, on occasion, the French and English.

Handsome Lake was born in 1735 in the Seneca village of Gonawagas on the Genesee River opposite the present town of Avon, Livingston County, New York State. By the time he reached his forties, the Iroquoian nation was deprived of its military ardour, reduced to political impotence, corrupted in its customs, disillusioned with its religion, stripped of its hunting land, and made to look depraved and contemptible in the eyes of both white and native neighbours.

It is known from tradition and from his own story that Handsome Lake became a dissolute person and a miserable victim of alcohol. For four years he was a helpless invalid. It was during this time that he was visited by three celestial beings and given the Good Message. He was past the prime of life and weakened by disease and drunkenness, yet he accepted the role of teacher and prophet for his people. The model of a sufferer of afflictions, Handsome Lake became a beacon of hope with his divine message. The *Gaiwí:yo*. In spite of his past, he became a commanding figure. He created a new system — something to think about, to discuss, to believe. The success of Handsome Lake's teachings did much to establish the Iroquois as a distinct social group.

It is never easy for a white person to attempt to understand the native way, just as it is not easy for a native to understand the thinking of a white person. We are different. The native elders speak of honouring all things, and they have no word for "why." There is no need to ask "why" because they accept what is the Great Mystery. White people, on the other hand, always want to solve the mystery.

As a young boy, Chief Jacob Thomas learned the Code of Handsome Lake by attending the Longhouse and hearing the Good Word of the Code recited twice a year by an elder. His father, Chief David Thomas, reminded him to always attend and to listen closely to the words of the elders. Chief Thomas obeyed his father and today he is a spokesman, orator, and elder for his people. He lives by the Code and reminds his people to honour the ways of their forefathers, to learn the Code, and to speak their native languages. As an elder and faithkeeper, he continues to work and teach native and non-native people the need to live with a good mind.

Chief Jacob Thomas has certainly proved this to be true in his life. He has spent the last thirty years lecturing about his teachings and demonstrating his skills in traditional crafts throughout North America. In 1973 Jake was hired as assistant professor of Iroquois culture and traditions and of oral Mohawk language at Trent University in Peterborough, Ontario, and worked there until his retirement in 1990. His woodcarvings of masks, condolence canes, ceremonial effigy bowls, and blackash splint baskets are in private and public collections around the world, including the collection of Prince Charles of England.

I gave Chief Jacob Thomas honest answers to the questions he had about what was involved in writing a book and how we might accomplish it. I told him I felt it was important for him to tell his story to his people and to non-native society. It also seemed important to find an Iroquoian illustrator, and we were fortunate to connect readily with Randell Hill.

Mr. Hill lives at Ohsweken, Six Nations, near Brantford, Ontario. As a self-taught artist, Randell has developed many aspects of his creative potential. The illustrations he conceived and subsequently created to expand the text of the Code reflect considerable power of vision and the gift of a real artist. His sensitivity to the words of the text was no doubt greatly assisted by his keen sense of co-operation and willingness. It was a pleasure and a revelation to share some time and space with him.

Teachings from the Longhouse not only represents traditional beliefs but also speaks of living in harmony within community, as symbolized by the longhouse building itself. This traditional Iroquois dwelling was dark, noisy, and smoke-filled. It was a rectangular, gable-roofed structure measuring anywhere from fifty to seventy-five feet in length. The longhouse was constructed of sheets of elm bark lashed onto stout poles, housing up to fifty or sixty people.

The inhabitants of a longhouse were usually kinfolk of one clan — theoretically, the multifamily residence of maternal lineage. The dwelling could be inhabited by an old woman, her female descendants, together with their husbands and the children, and any unmarried sons. The totem animal of the clan to which the lineage belonged — Deer, Bear, Wolf, Snipe, or whatever it might be — was carved above the door. This totem attached to the longhouse not only represented the occupants, but also provided a stranger with the information needed to seek out hospitality or aid in the village.

The longhouse emphasized a need to care for family and friends. From the outside it may have appeared to be a structure to keep the elements out or to provide warmth on a frigid night, but each patch of elm bark on this home represented love and devotion to caring for the needs of family and the community. The people of the Iroquois Confederacy led a communal existence.

The term Longhouse, used in its religious sense, includes the council house, or Longhouse, where people assemble to discuss politics and war and peace or to worship the Great Spirit. The interior is sparsely furnished. At each end of the Longhouse there are two tiers of raised, grand-stand-like benches, and there are two similar tiers along the sides. Moveable wooden benches stand in front of the fixed seating tiers and are arranged in various ways, depending on the use to which the Longhouse is being put. In the centre of the floor there is a bench for drummers to sit on when there is dancing. It seemed to me that Chief Thomas and I could be like the Longhouse. We could, metaphorically speaking, get under one roof and live and honour the teachings together in a right way in book form. He needed a writer and I was ready for the teaching.

In preparing this text of the Code of Handsome Lake,

we used a script written in 1918, which came from the oral tradition in the Onondaga language. Chief Jacob Thomas had already transcribed the script into English, but the text was not expanded, and it was not in circulation as a published work. He had done the translation for the benefit of his people who no longer spoke their native language. As we worked together on his text, we also incorporated some of the material gathered and printed in 1912 by A.C. Parker under the title *The Code of Handsome Lake, The Seneca Prophet.*

Our journey together with this book has been a very moving experience. His words have given me much thought and emotion; we have laughed together and listened hard to one another: we have remained in agreement and worked patiently for clarity. We both knew in our hearts that the Creator had brought us together for this reason.

In this new era of cultural interchange and integration, it is difficult to be clear about relationships. People attempt to move with teachings from another culture without taking the time to first learn to think in the way of the other culture. Have we forgotten the ways of wisdom, the work and self-discipline needed to reach full understanding and working of knowledge?

People everywhere are searching for something that will help their lives and their world to make sense. They need to realize their purpose in life and find their true direction. This text will give much to those who are seeking their purpose and to those who are already following their true direction. The information contained in this book includes principles that need to be considered for natives and non-natives to develop a good mind, to honour all things, and to practise no criticism and no judgement.

Teachings from the Longhouse represents a message to all people living on the Earth Mother, a message of keeping a good mind, and of respecting life and caring for others. We are indeed fortunate to have this wisdom made available to us today. It is truly amazing that despite the hardships suffered by the native peoples, an elder should come forth to share a message that will benefit all people.

It is in this sharing and true understanding that we may all behave and live as good human beings. As Chief Thomas would say, "We need to be better human beings and not say I am better than anyone else, but try to be better within oneself."

My work with native teachers over the years has helped me to rekindle the fire of my purpose and to honour the gift with which I have been blessed. *Teachings from the Longhouse* was a journey and a movement in self-discipline for me. It is a way of life for Chief Jacob Thomas of the Six Nations.

I thank you, Jake.

TERRY BOYLE
Parry Sound, Ontario
January 1994

A Faithkeeper
Speaks His Truth

THE MORNING WAS still young. Bright rays of sunshine burst through the tops of the old maple trees surrounding our century-old white clapboard home in the village of Prince Albert, Ontario. A gentle knock at the back door indicated the arrival of a visitor. I was well aware who that visitor was, but unsure of my approach.

As I opened the door, my breath was cut short as a quiet voice uttered, "Hello." It was Chief Jacob Thomas.

He was of medium height and wore a brown sports jacket neatly tailored to fit his slim frame. He grinned from the corner of his mouth, exchanging a greeting with a twinkle in his eyes. The motion of spirit and the depth of insight in those eyes was easily felt. The shiny bolo tie he wore suddenly caught my eye — I regained my composure and invited him in. We shook hands and began our journey together into a world of native spiritual enlightenment.

Chief Thomas is a natural-born craftsman and historian who has carried on the oral traditions of his forefathers. This seventy-two-year-old man has learned many things from his grandfather, David Skye, and his father, David Thomas, both Onondaga chiefs. His grandmother, Julia Thomas, who raised him, was a medicine woman. In 1973 Chief Thomas was condoled as a Cayuga chief of the Six Nations.

The Condolence Ceremony is deeply rooted in the epic founding of the Iroquois Confederacy, a mythic drama pitting the forces of war and destruction against the discipline of the "good mind," with its code of "peace, power, and righteousness." The ancient ritual of the Condolence is a protocol of greetings, condoling, and most of all, renewal, after the death of a chief or other tribal member.

Before we started our interview for the book, Jake walked around our studio space. He examined the native art, wall hangings, and drums that decorated the barnboard beams. He might have been studying the artwork, but I knew instinctively that he was really touching in with the vibrations of our home. His grin reappeared as he turned to take a seat at the dining-room table.

Lighting up a cigarette and puffing out a volume of smoke that engulfed both of us, the chief contemplated his words. In a soft voice he began his story by telling me that the Ongwehónwe (the native peoples, meaning, literally, "the real person") have lived on Turtle Island (North America), according to their tradition, since the Creator placed them there. At that time, he also gave them the responsibilities of caring for Mother Earth, commanded respect from them for the animals and plant kingdoms, and counselled co-operation for survival among humans. The Iroquoian-speaking peoples of North America include the Cherokee from the Southern Appalachian area; the Tuscarora and the

Susquehanna of the mid-Atlantic region; and the Huron, Wenro, Erie, Tobacco, Mohawk, Oneida, Onondaga, Cayuga, and Seneca of the Great Lakes – St. Lawrence River Valley regions of North America. The last five nations — the Mohawk, Oneida, Onondaga, Cayuga, and Seneca — are the best known of all the Iroquois, because of the alliance, or Confederacy, that they formed, known as The League of the Hotinonshón:ni (the People of the Longhouse). The Tuscaroras joined the Iroquois Confederacy in 1724 and became the sixth nation. The Hotinonshón:ni peoples practised agriculture and hunting and had extensive trade routes.

Chief Jacob Thomas pointed out that each time a major period of social unrest caused dissension within the community, a prophet would rise up to guide the people and reveal the will of the Creator to achieve a harmonious, healthy society.

For example, when intertribal wars threatened the survival of the Five Nations, the Peacemaker and his spokesman Hayenhwátha created the Confederacy with its Great Law of Peace. When disease, famine, and spiritual despair threatened the Ongwehónwe, the Fatherless Man gave the people the Thanksgiving Ceremonies and the practices of medicine. Finally, when alcohol and the invasion of white people caused social and political upheaval, Handsome Lake was given a message by four celestial beings.

To offer a better understanding of the traditions of the Six Nations, Chief Thomas talks about the Peacemaker and the Great Law. The Peacemaker was born in a Huron village near the Bay of Quinte, on the north shore of Lake Ontario. This baby was born with a name, but the native people today know him only as the Peacemaker. His arrival had been announced to a young virgin woman in a dream. In this dream, a spirit messenger from the Creator (He-who-made-you) told her that she would bear a son who would be named "Deganawída"; he would be a messenger of the Creator and he would bring peace and harmony to the people on Earth.

When the Peacemaker became a man, he said one day to his mother, "I shall now build my canoe from this white stone, for the time has come for me to start my mission in this world. I know I must travel afar on lakes and rivers to seek out the council smoke of nations beyond this lake. It is now time for me to go and stop the shedding of blood among human beings." The Hotinonshón:ni (or People of the Longhouse) were at war with one another. The Peacemaker's mission in life was to bring peace, power, and righteousness to all nations.

Jake tells this story to highlight the journey of the Peacemaker. "On his journey, the Peacemaker met a cannibal. He saw what the cannibal was doing but he did not come there because the cannibal was eating human flesh. He did not say as we say today. "If you don't do what is right, then I'm going to kill you. If you don't do what I say, then I'm going to punish you." The Peacemaker at the time did not want to kill or punish the cannibal. He did know the cannibal was killing people, but the cannibal did not know what the Creator had intended. The cannibal did not know any better.

So when the Peacemaker arrived at the cannibal's lodge, he saw human bones scattered all around his home. Now the Peacemaker knew he had been sent by the Creator and was meant to approach this cannibal. Arriving at the front door, he quickly realized that the cannibal was not at home. So he climbed up onto the longhouse roof and lay down on the roof by the smoke hole. In a short time the cannibal returned, carrying a human body. He took the body inside the long-house and began to chop it up into smaller portions of meat and put them in a pot to boil.

Soon the meat was cooked and the cannibal reached over and removed the pot from the fire to allow the meat to cool down. When he thought the meat was cool enough to eat, he got up and walked over to the pot and leaned over to scoop the meat out. He looked down into the pot and saw a face appear in it. He looked again and thought to himself that he had never seen a face in the pot before. He stood back and began to wonder what was happening. He thought for a little while and realized maybe it was just his eyes playing tricks on him. He looked into the pot again and saw the face once again. Now he was really confused. He sat down and thought how beautiful the face was that he saw in the pot. It was a handsome face. He wondered if he had a face that looked so handsome and why would he eat such flesh. Now the good mind was beginning to work. He started to think that what he was doing was wrong. He thought for a little longer and said to himself, "Maybe it is wrong what I am doing."

A third time he returned for another look in the pot. He saw the face again and this time realized that what he was doing was wrong. He decided the time had come to quit eating human flesh. The cannibal then took the pot and carried it outside and down the hill to the place where a tree had fallen and a cavern appeared in the earth. He took the meat out of the pot and dumped it into the hole in the ground. Then as the cannibal turned to walk back to the longhouse, he met the Peacemaker. "Who are you and where do you come from?" the cannibal asked. "I come from the west," the Peacemaker replied. "I am just passing through."

"What is your name?" the cannibal asked.

"My name is the Peacemaker," he replied.

The cannibal continues by asking, "What is your purpose?"

The Peacemaker answered, "My purpose is to ask you what you buried down at the bottom of the hill."

"I just buried some human flesh," the cannibal said. "When I was cooking the meat as I have always done, I saw a beautiful face. Every time I went back to the pot and looked down, I saw this face. The third time this happened to me, I decided I was going to quit my habit and not eat human meat again."

"That is why I am here," the Peacemaker said, "to do away with these evil practices."

The cannibal asked the Peacemaker to return to his longhouse so they could talk some more. Once inside, the Peacemaker asked the cannibal to make a fire and boil some water. While the cannibal was busy building the fire, the Peacemaker left and went hunting and returned with a deer. The Peacemaker then asked the cannibal to work with him. This would demonstrate to the cannibal that working together meant sharing a good mind.

He then told the cannibal that they were going to skin this animal. While they did this, he talked about the Creator telling the cannibal that he had been given the deer to eat, instead of human flesh. They talked about developing a good mind and how important it was for other people to develop a good mind that would result in peace, power, and righteousness. The Peacemaker went on to say that when you work together, you exemplify peace, which in turn results in power of mind.

They sat for a while and talked about the next day. The Peacemaker said, "When the sun comes up next day, it will get brighter and brighter and bring warmth and comfort to the people. That sun will bring a good mind, and as it continues to rise, it will be a symbol of peace to all nations."

Chief Thomas concludes by telling how the Peacemaker managed to bring all the league of the Hotinónshon꞉ni (the Iroquois Nations) together. When he did this, he addressed the people, saying, "Each nation must select a certain number of their wisest and kindest men to be the chiefs. These men will be the advisers of the people. They will sit in the Council of the League and make the decisions for their respected nations. The women holding the hereditary titles* will make the selections and the confirmations. Once named, the chiefs shall be crowned with deer antlers to symbolize their positions."

The Mohawk women titleholders brought forth nine men for chiefs; next, the Oneida women titleholders brought

---

*   The Iroquois were described as matriarchal because of the important role women played in the formal political organization. They exercised political power in three main circumstances. First, whenever one of the forty-nine chiefs of the great intertribal League of the Iroquois died, the senior women of his lineage nominated his successor. Second, when tribal or village decisions had to be made, both men and women attended a village meeting, and while men were the chiefs and normally did the public speaking, the women caucused behind the scenes and lobbied with the spokesmen. Third, a woman was entitled to demand publicly that a murdered kinsman or kinswoman be replaced by a captive from a non-Iroquois tribe. The Iroquois women were entitled formally to select chiefs, to participate in consensual politics, and to start wars. They also maintained genealogical and political continuity in a matrilineal system in which the primary kin relationship was the one between mother and daughter.

forward nine men for chiefs; then the Onondaga women brought forth fourteen men to become chiefs; then the Seneca women brought forth eight men to become chiefs; and finally, the Cayuga women brought forth ten men to become chiefs. After this ceremony took place, each chief was then responsible for delivering a string of wampum,* one span of the hand in length, to the Peacemaker, as a pledge of truthfulness and sincerity.

Now the Peacemaker spoke to the chiefs and those people assembled. He explained that these men would no longer have the same names but greater ones. They would each have antlers as a symbol of their position. In their position, they would receive much abuse, he said, and the thickness of their skin must be seven spans of the hand. Each of them must work for the people. There must be unity so that no one could hurt one nation without hurting all nations. They must always think in terms of the generations to come. Their authority would come from the Great Peace which each nation had pledged to uphold.

The Binding Law (the Great Law of Peace) was then devised by the Peacemaker and read, and the Iroquois Confederacy was established. The Great Law wampum belts described the various functions of the people and the rules they should follow according to the law.

A tree of peace was planted. From the tree grew four roots — one extending north, one south, one east, and one west. They were called the Great White Roots

---

* Wampum is a kind of cylindrical bead, perforated through from one or both ends and threaded into strings or woven into geometrically patterned belts. The geometrical patterns conveyed messages by use of symbol. The wampum belts also represented agreements such as treaties and marriages.

(*Oktehagenhtgó:wa*), symbolizing peace and charity. If any nation or individual from outside adopted the Great Law, then upon learning it or by tracing the roots to the Great Tree, they would discipline their minds and spirits to obey and honour the wishes of the Council of the League. Then they will be made welcome to take shelter under the branches of this tree.

It was said that an eagle would sit at the top of the tree to see far into the distance. Should any danger ever threaten the lives of the Hotinonshón:ni (the People of the Longhouse) an eagle would immediately warn of its approach.

Five bound arrows symbolized the complete union. This represented the power of one with the Hotinonshón:ni, and it showed that they had bound themselves together in one head, one body, one spirit, and one soul to settle all matters.

A pine tree was pulled out by its roots, and into the depth of the hole that the roots left they threw all their weapons of war. They were swept into strong currents of water and carried to areas unknown. The Hotinonshón:ni then replaced the pine tree, completing the burial of their weapons of war, hiding them from sight to help establish the Great Law.

When the Europeans arrived, the Hotinonshón:ni had only one belief, the Great Law. Gradually, however, people once again took different directions of understanding and went back to practising the old ways that had existed before the formation of the League. They had done away with the warring and fighting and killing, but now these practices had returned.

According to Chief Thomas, "The eyes of the Creator were saddened by what people were doing. The people had returned to witchcraft and to not caring for one another. Worse yet, the Europeans had brought with them many things to weaken and disorganize the people. The oral tradition was threatened, and the Creator was trying to find a prophet to bring the message back to the people.

"The Creator tried to deliver a message to the people that he was sad about the Europeans bringing alcohol, which would ruin their lives. There was no control, although they had leaders at that time to keep people in order because no force was used. Europeans have police, judges, lawyers, and the jails, but the Iroquois Nations never had that. We never had that because we did not place judgement on individuals. It was not our place to judge anyone because we all have faults, and if we started judging others, they would ask us about our faults: That is the reason why we do not have judges among our own people. We cannot take life away. The white man created his own way of punishment. That is why you have hell on earth today. If you disobey the white man's law, you are sent away to hell."

Chief Jacob Thomas states, "This Good Message would allow the Ongwehónwe to survive as a people and as a nation. The message included instructions on how to live a good life, maintain the family unit, provide for young and old, and contribute to the stability and well-being of the community."

As the Good Message was preached on an annual basis and its tenets adhered to by the communities, it began to assume the structure of a religion, a formal system of belief and practice. When the American War of Independence divided the Iroquoian community, the Code of Handsome Lake remained a unifying factor.

The Good Message (which also came to be known as the Code of Handsome Lake) is a belief for all people to live by and reminds us how we should conduct ourselves and behave like good human beings. It also tells us how we should care for and respect one another and our elders.

Chief Jacob Thomas continued by adding, "The Code speaks of alcohol, love medicine, witchcraft, and abortion. The teachings cover all prophecies. The prophecies spoken in the Code of Handsome Lake pertain to events occurring today in our world."

Chief Thomas paused for a moment and looked out the window to view the landscape. I suddenly realized that I was no longer interviewing him, instead he was beginning to teach me. My questions became more infrequent as he spoke what was on his mind.

He went on to say, "I was brought up by my parents in the traditional native way. When they disciplined me, they made me aware that there were limitations to what I could do. I was always told about what could happen in my lifetime if I didn't listen to them. My parents always told me that there was a devil who could lead my life if I listened to the many things that could lead me into trouble — such as drinking alcohol, murder, gambling, stealing, and not being honest with people. I was told that if I did any of those things, I would end up in prison for life. They tried to tell me about the traditional teachings of the Code of Handsome Lake.

As I grew older, I understood more about what my parents had told me over and over again. I am thankful that I was taught about Handsome Lake's Code. That is still what I believe in and that is what makes me what I am today. I work to be a better human being. This is not to say that I am better than anyone else, but rather that I try to be better within myself. I also learned to preach the Code myself — to my people who are still the followers of Handsome Lake."

The text which follows is Chief Jacob Thomas's rendition of the *Gaiwí:yo*, the Good Message, or Code of Handsome Lake.

The Code of Handsome Lake

*Our story begins on the Allegheny River at a place called
"Ohio" (New York State), also known as Burnt House, or
Dyononhsadé:genh.*

TOWARDS THE END of the 1700s, the Iroquois Confederacy began to deteriorate. Although the Confederacy
had protected their territory from the Dutch, English,
French, and the Thirteen Colonies (which later became
the United States of America), their population was down
to one-quarter of what it had been when white people had
first arrived. Diseases to which they had no immunity —
like measles, chicken pox, and smallpox — had swept
through their villages. In 1779 the American General John
Sullivan destroyed the basis of Iroquois power by burning
their villages and cornfields and destroying a large number
of the warehouses that held their food supplies. The
Hotinónshon:ni saw their territories decreasing and many
of them turned to the fur trade for survival.

In those days, many people would gather after the harvest and at this meeting a leader would decide when it was time for the men to go to their winter hunting places. After they had set a time, the men and their leader would prepare their canoes. Then they would take half the harvest and leave the other half for the people who remained in the village. When they arrived at their hunting place, they took great care to store their canoes, making them safe, so that the ice on the river would not damage them. They would walk into the woods and make camp, for they knew what to expect from the winter there. The men were very fortunate that the winter hunting and trapping often brought great bounty. The leader, who always watched the weather, would send a runner to check the river. When the ice on the river went down and it was safe to travel, the hunters would prepare to leave, putting all their game into the canoe and heading upstream to a settlement called Pittsburgh in what is now Pennsylvania.

Once they arrived in Pittsburgh, the first thing they did was trade furs for kegs of rum and whiskey. As they started on their journey home, they would start drinking. They tied their canoes together, making a raft or barge, so that they continued to paddle together, but they would get so drunk that some of them would fall out of their canoes and drown. This would go on until they reached their village. Meanwhile, the people who remained in the village would hear their hunters returning from trading the hides and would gather all the children and run down to the shore, meet the canoes, and help them unload the whiskey and rum.

For a number of days a huge party would take place until all the alcohol was gone. Sometimes some of the people would run away into the woods, returning to the village days later only to find bodies lying here and there. Some of the people would be hurt, some would be passed out, others would have been killed during the course of the drinking. When this was all over, the people would bury the dead, clean up, and try to start over.

Sganyadaí:yoh (Handsome Lake) was a member of the Seneca Nation who lived during this time. He had been born in 1735 in the Seneca village of Ganawágas on the Genesee River. He held a Seneca sachem* for his people. As sachem, he represented the honourable position of leadership of his nation.

Sganyadaí:yoh was a heavy drinker, one of alcohol's many victims, and his people saw their leader's suffering. His daughter took care of him so he could rest and recover from his illness. He was sick for a period of four years and had to be confined to his bed.

During a time when he was feeling better than usual, he began thinking of his position as chief in the Confederacy — and then he thought about the way he had been carrying on. Many times as he lay there, he looked up through the smoke hole in the roof to the outside. Seeing the top of the trees and the stars in the sky, he started to think and asked himself, "Where did all this come from? Why is this all here? What am I doing here? What does this all mean?"

Sganyadaí:yoh started remembering all the things that he had heard since he was a young boy. How some day the white's firewater would destroy all of them. He began to remember who he was and what his relationship was to Shongwàyadíhs:on (the Creator — literally, "He who made you"), so each morning he started to give thanks for having seen another day. As he lay there looking through the smoke

---

* The title "sachem" means a leader of his people or chief of a nation.

hole, he thought, Maybe this lifestyle I have been living is wrong, is not getting me or my people anywhere.

Every time Sganyadaí:yoh started thinking good thoughts, he began to feel better. And as he started to feel better, his strength returned. He lay in bed for four years and started to think more clearly about who he was and why he was here. As he started to recover and gain strength, he gave thanks.

Now he realized he had to make a decision, that he had better quit for good and start thinking of his people, his relationship with Shongwàyadíhs:on, and how his nation would survive.

One June morning, as the dew was beginning to dry,

Sganyadaí:yoh awoke. His daughter and her husband, sitting outside by the doorway cleaning beans for planting, heard him stir. His daughter turned to look at the door and saw her father standing at the doorway. When he collapsed, she was so frightened that she yelled to her husband, "Go and tell my uncle Cornplanter (Gayentwágeh) that his brother looks like he has passed away." So her husband rushed over to Cornplanter's, then to his nephew Black Snake. Cornplanter said, "As soon as I am finished covering the seeds, I will be over."

Black Snake was the first to arrive. He went straight to his uncle's bedside, examined him, and felt his chest. He found a warm spot on his uncle's chest. The people were already assembled and had begun mourning, thinking that the great leader was gone. They started making burial arrangements, dressing Sganyadaí:yoh in his finest traditional clothes.

But Black Snake said, "Be patient, we will wait. Do not grieve." About mid-morning, the people suddenly noticed that the great leader had opened his eyes and was moving his lips. It was as if he had just awakened. Then Black Snake said to his uncle, "How are you?"

His uncle was not able to answer him. All he could do was move his lips. He was unable to say a word. Again it looked as if he went back to sleep.

It was just about noon when he began to move and open his eyes. Again Black Snake said to his uncle, "How are you feeling?" This time Sganyadaí:yoh was able to speak.

He told the gathering, "I saw some very bright sunlight with great colours, more brilliant than ever before. It was very good to be there. I heard a voice as I lay in bed. A man asked me to come outside. He called me a second time but I knew I couldn't move, for I had not moved in a long time. I tried to sit up, even though I knew that I couldn't. But I found that I was able to stand and walk and step outside.

"Then I saw three men standing off a little way and one called to me. These men all looked the same. They were very beautiful, very handsome, their faces were painted. Each one carried a bow and arrows in one hand and elderberry branches in the other. I had never seen anyone look as they did. It seemed as if their feet were not touching the ground. They told me, 'Our feet never touch the ground.' They were sent to Earth by Shongwàyadíhs:on to look for a certain strongminded man who was doing wrong. This man had to repent for using ohné:gah (alcohol).

"I said to them, 'I have been hoping, if it would be possible, to walk again on Earth. I repent that I sang the Ohgí:weh (the Death Chant or the Ghost Dance) songs. The quivering songs and dances have brought evil to my life and made me do wrong things.'

"Then the Three Messengers said, 'We think there are some other things that Shongwayàdíhs:on wants to hear.'

"I said, 'I am hoping the Great Spirit may let me walk again on Earth. I now repent of all the evil things I have done and I also repent of using alcohol, which made Shongwayàdíhs:on sad.'

"Then the messengers said to me, 'That is what He wanted to hear. So now He has heard it all. So He who created you has decided that He is going to give you strength and power. He will let you walk again on Earth. He has appointed you to do some important things for Him. So this is what will be done: There are two medicine people, a man and a wife, among you who will prepare medicine for you. Their names are Ojiskwá:then: and Gayengó:gwas. They will go into the woods early in the morning and pick the medicine. This native medicine will be prepared for you to drink for three days. If you are unable to use it up by the third morning, then the rest can be cast away. When they have made this medicine for you, then you will be isolated for three days.

"'The people shall pick strawberries early in the morning and make it into a strawberry drink. People shall assemble in the Longhouse and the leaders shall appoint two men to serve the drink, and each person shall give thanksgiving. They shall not say that you are fortunate you recovered, but shall say that *we* are very fortunate you have recovered.' The messengers said, 'This will help you regain your strength.'

"'Never let us hear your relations say, "He is poor and fortunate to walk again on Earth." Whenever your relations mention this, they will say, "We are fortunate he rose again and walked on Earth."

"'Your relations will assemble in the Longhouse tomorrow morning and then you will see them. The ceremony will begin at noontime. The ceremony will continue with the Great Dance, the Feather Dance. It is necessary to have the strawberry drink prepared because this is what we give thanks with. The strawberry drink will be served and each person will give thanks.'"

The people gathered and did as they were instructed. Many people were there, and when Sganyadaí:yoh approached them, some were sad. His daughter helped him as they prepared for the Great Feather Dance.

When it was over and everything that the messengers had requested was completed, he told the people of his vision. He said, "The messengers were sent by Shongwayàdíhs:on to tell the people on Earth that they were not aware of wrong-doing — and because the Creator had given thanksgiving and renewal to Sganyadaí:yoh after he repented of his wrongdoing, they had chosen him to be the one to bring the Good Message (or *Gaiwí:yo*) of Shongwayàdíhs:on (the Creator's highest code of ethics)."

THE MESSAGE OF THE FOUR CELESTIAL BEINGS

The Three Messengers spoke to Sganyadaí:yoh (Handsome Lake) and through him relayed the messages of Shongwayàdíhs:on, the Creator. They spoke about the present happenings as well as the future. They spoke about good and evil and the need for good personal conduct. They spoke about the things that we had left behind and the things that we had adopted which were not meant for our people.

The messengers told Sganyadaí:yoh that they would come to him from time to time to speak of events that needed to be told to the people. They said that there were four of them but that the fourth messenger would meet him later. (At the time, the fourth messenger had gone over the Great Saltwater [the Atlantic Ocean] to relate their prophecy to the white people there.)

"So now we will offer the message to you and you will tell it truly before all the people. No matter how wicked your life has been, you have now put all this aside. We will be guiding you. It is through you that we will speak to the people. We will uncover the evil upon the earth and show how people have gone astray from the laws that Shongwayàdíhs:on had laid down for the Ongwehónwe. All this is now prepared for you to truthfully tell to all the people."

◈

THE FOUR MAJOR MATTERS
The First Matter
"Deganigonhadé:nyons," Meaning "Mind Changer"

We will start with what has made our Creator, Shongwayàdíhs:on, most sad, the substance the people here on Earth enjoy using. What you call *"deganigonhadé:nyons"* is what the messengers call the "mind changer" and was not given to the Ongwehónwe. This is what made the Creator feel sad when your relations delighted in consuming strong drink. It is not for your relations to use. He did not give it to your people. He gave it to your white brothers, the white-skinned people. He gave it to them because of the work they have to do, and it should be taken only three times a day, once in the morning, once at noon, and once in the evening. It was only to be used as medicine, but they have abused it, and it will cause many minds to split, and many will die from it.

For the Ongwehónwe it will bring great misery and hardship. When you have touched the firewater, you will like it. But you must remember what will result from drinking it. Anyone who has drunk the firewater will know it as the "mind changer." These people must reaffirm their faith and renewal to Shongwayàdíhs:on and pledge never to touch the firewater again.

The Second Matter
"Góhtgon," Meaning *"Witchcraft"*

*Now we will tell you and your relations of another practice
which makes Shongwayàdíhs:on sad.*

People who are not in their right minds make and spread disease to people through witchcraft,* causing death and cutting off the

---

* Witchcraft was introduced to the Iroquois by an Algonquin tribe that they had adopted — the Algonquins' early legends and traditions contain many allusions to witches and witchcraft.

Witches use at least two distinct methods to accomplish their ends. The first, thought to be the older way, is creating terrifying or harmful images in a person's mind by way of mental suggestion, either verbal or telepathic. Such witches were able to assume the form of ancient monsters, the *Nyágwai,* or mammoth bear, being the favourite form. They had the power of transforming people into beasts and of imprisoning them in trees without destroying the human nature or sensibilities of their victims.

The second and modern class of witches works evil spells by introducing into the bodies of their victims by supernatural means a small, needle-like splinter that is pointed at either end and has a central eye to which are tied the hair of the witch, a splinter of bone from the femur of a deer, and a worm or some similar object. Instances where such things have been drawn from bewitched persons are commonly reported.

A witch can work fearlessly and successfully as long as he or she remains unknown to number of days that Shongwayàdíhs: on has given to each of you. Many engage in this evil practice, called witchcraft. Witchcraft happens when people lose the control of their minds or thoughts. Again, witchcraft has made Him sad, and He is hoping you will cease this evil practice and never take it up again.

---

the victim and even, in some circumstances, when he or she is known. A "witched" person is often able to see, as in a vision, the witch wherever she goes, and is likewise able to tell when she is about to approach the house.

Witches fear any angry person who threatens to kill them. Such a threat, if it is an earnest one, is an effectual charm against further annoyance. To burn the object that a witch has introduced into one's body will torture the witch and kill her. Such objects are not often burned. If revenge is desired, the victim, if sufficiently angry, can throw the object through space and injure the witch wherever he or she wishes. People who successfully resist and destroy another witch's power may become witches if they so desire.

To torture a witch, force a confession, and exact a promise of repentance, a person must take a living bird, black in colour, and carry it into the woods at midnight. Here they must build a small fire, then split open the bird's body, extract its beating heart, and hang it by its cords over the fire to roast slowly. The witch will then exert every possible means to reach the spot and beg that the heart be taken from the fire before it is consumed. At such a time, any promise may be exacted, for the witch is powerless. If the heart is consumed, the witch will die of a "burnt heart."

Witch poison may be extracted by putting fine, sifted ashes on the afflicted part and staying in bed until the poison comes out. The charm will then be found in the ashes.

The spirits of great witches are able to return and possess another witch, and a witch who has such a "friend" is especially favoured. In time of need, the spirit-witch will direct her to money, goods, or food. Witches do not always injure people who have offended them; more often they injure their children or other near relatives. This is done so that the person they want to punish may see an innocent person suffer for their offence and so be tortured all the more.

Witch doctors are of two classes: witches, who are willing to pit their powers against other witches, and medicine men, who have made a special study of the charms that will offset witches' spells. This class also has two divisions: those who make a regular profession of dispelling witch influences, of discovering the causes of mysterious ailments, of extracting the object that causes the trouble, and of identifying witches, as well as those who by reason of some special service they have rendered some spirit of nature, have been rewarded with magical powers, great wisdom, and immunity from malefic influences. This class renders its services freely.

The wearing of small false faces and frequent invocations of the Thunder spirit, accompanied by liberal offerings of tobacco, are potent charms against witches. The False Face Society has an annual ceremony in which witch spirits are expelled from the community. The Hennahí:das Society is said to be the surviving remnant of an older witch society introduced among the Seneca by the Nanticoke. Its members are reputed to possess magic powers.

Even now we notice that someone is thinking of this evil practice. Shongwayàdís:on has given everyone a certain number of days to live, but evil has interfered with and shortened some people's lives or cut off Shongwayàdís:on's creation. In these cases, his creation (a human being) has not reached his or her set time to become an adult, bear children, and reach old age.

So now we tell you what they must do. They must go into the woods alone and offer tobacco to Shongwayàdíhs:on and ask for forgiveness. They must vow to live pure lives and give thanksgiving to Shongwayàdíhs:on so that their lives may never again be as they were in the past.

The Third Matter
"Onón:hweht," Meaning "Love Medicine"

Now we will tell you and your relations of another evil practice that the people on Earth engage in. It is this third word that makes Shongwayàdíhs:on sad.

There are a great number of people who use this medicine to control the lives of other people. This is a medicine charm* that has caused much misery. It is wrong to

---

* Should a person die holding the secret of a charm, one may discover it by sleeping on the ground with a handful of the grave dirt beneath his head. Then, if all conditions are perfect, the dead person will appear in three successive visions and reveal the mystery. The most effective charm for drawing riches is the tooth of a *Nyágwai* (the bear).

Diviners of mysteries have always been prominent among native people. Their office is to tell their clients the medicine society that would be most efficacious in curing the sick, to discover the whereabouts of lost children or articles, to discover what witch was working her spells, and to tell fortunes, as well as to interpret dreams.

practise evil medicine secretly. A person who means to give it up forever must be sincere and truthful. Such practices are evil, and the Creator hopes that wicked people who carry them out will repent of them as long as they may live.

Many of your relations have practised this evil thing. They have learned about administering love potions on one another. We call it "submission medicine" because it conquers and hypnotizes the mind. Your relations do not realize that many people have died because of this practice. It has destroyed many people. A great number of your relations have practised it, and the Creator is sad because of the great wrong they have done.

Tell your relatives that those who have administered love potions must repent of this wrongdoing at once and make their repentance everlasting all the days that they live on Earth. If anyone fails to repent on Earth, they will follow the wide path that leads to the House of Punishment.

If a person has learned the powers of curing a person ailing from witch potions, then she should do so without charge at any time. We feel this would be helpful to your relations. This is the way we look at things: Whenever your relations charge for preparing medicine for others, it is wrong, because a person may be so sick that she cannot afford to pay. The Creator has given each person a gift and talent in order to help others. Your relations should not accept any kind of pay because this is the right way.

If individuals are helpful and generous, they will earn a reward from the Creator.

The Fourth Matter
"Gódadwiyahdon:donh," Meaning "Abortion"

*Now we will tell you and your relations about the fourth word
that makes Shongwayàdíhs:on sad.*

It was Shongwayàdíhs:on's intention for women to give
birth to children. Some women always want to look their
best, so they cut off the life strings of the children.*
Shongwayàdíhs:on made women so that the generations
will be renewed. It means that we all live a certain length of
time and then pass on, making way for new generations. The
women are to have a certain number of children so they will
fulfill the will of Shongwayàdíhs:on.

They must pledge to Shongwayàdíhs:on that they will
always respect life for the sake of future generations. They
must give thanksgiving to Shongwayàdíhs:on, pledge forgiveness for past actions, and live according to his laws.

Now this is the way we see things among your relations.
Truly a woman bore and took care of her children. She suffered
much when giving birth to all her children, and when her
mother saw all her suffering, she prepared medicine** and
told her daughter its purpose. She prepared the medicine
for her to drink so she would never ever be pregnant
again.

The way we think and feel is that it was wrong for her

---

* The Seneca and Onondaga belief is that every woman has a certain number of children
predestined to her and that they are fastened on a string-like cord like tubers, or like eggs
in a bird.

** The Iroquois knew of such an herb used to prevent childbirth.

to accept the medicine. So the mother and the daughter were both doing wrong, a great wrong against the Creator.

So He ordained that the woman would give birth to a child anyway. She had a hard time giving birth but fortunately came through it. Then, as happened before, her mother prepared medicine for her daughter. She told her daughter, "The next time you give birth to a child, that may be the last of you. I want you to drink this medicine so you will never ever be with child again."

Now the daughter understood what her mother wanted her to do. So she said to her mother, "I want to do what is right for myself because the Creator wanted me to bring children into this world."

The messengers were listening to what the daughter said to her mother and related the message to Handsome Lake. They said, "We all heard what the daughter said to her mother and we are grateful and thank the girl. She did not take the medicine that her mother had prepared for her and has done a great thing for the Creator. This is the way he ordained, as a continuation of birth, and it is a great sin for any woman to cut off birth."

Marriage
(Ganáh:gwa)

This is what the messengers said the Creator intended marriage to be:

The way He intended and ordained things is that a man and woman should come together to raise children and love and care for them. He intended children to be born, replacing humankind for all time to come. Young people have no respect for marriage. The Creator's Law is broken when your relations live together for only a short time and then desert one another.

This is what made Shongwayàdíhs:on sad. So tell your relations not to give up hope but to try to live according to good conduct and honour the Good Message which you will be relating to them from time to time. There may be those who will say, "I am too sinful for the Creator to forgive me." They may think they have accumulated too much sin. A person should not think that way because the Creator is always waiting for a person to repent, so He will always reconsider.

The door is always open for individuals to repent to Him.

This part is what the messengers told Handsome Lake about a man and woman in marriage:

You will tell your relations that the tendency for mothers to breed mischief in marriages must stop. The marriage is to be discussed by the parents when the boy or girl in question grows up in the village. They will decide. The two mothers will talk about their son and daughter when they are old enough for marriage. The couple may marry only when the marriage is sanctioned by the parents. This is the way the Creator has ordained it.

He has created the two sexes — male and female — and He thought people should grow just like plants so there would always be new life. He intended that there would be a time of death for the man and the woman, and only death would separate them. They are to love and care for one another as long as they may live.

The way we see it, everything came about the right way. The boy and the girl grew up and became a married couple. But then the girl's mother began creating trouble between the man and wife. She told her daughter what to say, advising her to be angry when her husband came home. But when her husband arrived home, everything was all right. His wife was joyful and happy and had prepared food for him to eat. The way we see it, the girl's mother was likely unhappy about the way her daughter felt toward her husband. So the very first time she had a chance to speak to her daughter, she cried and said, "I am surprised at you. I don't believe you care for me at all."

So truly it happened that her daughter was angry at her husband, although she had no reason to be angry at him. He did not know what he might have done wrong. So it happened the way the old woman had planned and the couple separated. It did not happen the way the Creator had intended. He ordained that a man and woman would come together and only death would separate them.

So the messengers said, "This is a serious matter when anyone, elders or parents, are involved in the marriage of their daughters or sons. Differences can be worked out by the couple. So if anyone interferes and breaks up the marriage, we will say that it is a great sin and the Creator is sad because that is not the way He intended it to be. Anyone who has that kind of mind should repent to the Creator, Shongwayàdíhs:on."

Childbirth

*This part is what the messengers said about a woman bearing
ten to twelve children:*

There will always be new life renewing humankind for time
to come. The way He intended it, each woman will bear ten
to twelve children and then she will have done her duty.
Now if she wishes to have more children, she may do so,
depending on her health. If a woman wishes to continue to
bear more children, then medicine will have to be prepared
for her to give her strength. She will use this medicine.

We think and feel that whoever is able to bear that many
children is fortunate because she has fulfilled the rules of the
Creator. She does it truthfully and has repented of all her
sins on Earth.

So whoever fulfills the teachings of the Good Message
will see the land of the Creator.

If it happens that someone suffers and dies giving birth,
that person will have a clear path to the land of the Creator.

Family Relations

*This is what the messengers said about a man who
leaves three families:*

A man and woman lived together and lived happily. Then
the man noticed that his wife had become pregnant. The
man became angry with his wife. He became angry because
she made a little mistake by saying the wrong thing. At once
he left his wife and went elsewhere.

The day came when she was to give birth to the child. She gave birth without the father there and looked after the child herself.

Only a short time later, the man was looking for another woman. He found another woman and they came to live together. Again he did the same thing, looking for trouble with her and becoming angry as soon as he noticed that she was pregnant. She didn't know why he was acting that way or what had gone wrong. He left her. It seems that small matters had become big matters.

It happened the same way again a third time.

If a man leaves his third family, we think he will not be able to see the land of the Creator. Now the Creator wants this wrongdoing to stop and cease forever.

This is what the messengers said about a man who is very fond of his daughter:

A wife discovered that her husband really did care for and love his daughter and she became jealous of her daughter. She became nasty and ugly to her husband because she needed more attention. She thought, "He will never leave me, no matter how I treat him because he loves his child so."

Truly it happened that whenever she got into these ugly moods, he kept begging her not to be that way. But she kept passing her ugly moods on to him because of the child.

Then his mind was hurt. He thought, "She doesn't take pity on me because of the way she is carrying on."

Then his mind became evil. He gave up hope, for it seemed his wife would never change.

We feel that whenever a man is disgusted, he will make

up his mind and go away. So, truly, it did happen. He left his wife and child. He went away from home.

Now the mother was left alone to support the child.

Your relations will repent of this wrongdoing at once and make their repentance everlasting all the days that they live on Earth.

The Man Who Rejected the Message

This part is about a man who disrespects the Good Message:

As Handsome Lake was standing and preaching the Good Message early in the morning, a man came into the Longhouse and stood at the doorway while the great leader was talking. While the man was standing at the doorway of the Longhouse, he let out a loud fart (*ahennihdé:nih*) and then he went outside. By the time everything was over in the Longhouse, the news had spread, the people had heard.

The man did not return to the home where he lived, so the people began to wonder what had happened. The great leaders at that time decided they should make a search for him. Some people volunteered and the search began.

Still the people were unable to locate him in the afternoon. So by night the search party was called off until the next morning.

Early the next morning the search began again. It was noontime when they found him. He was sitting in the fork of a large tree situated in the marshes, eating snakes. The man had lost his mind. This took place in the village of Allegheny on a Seneca reservation.

That is what happened to the man who did not respect

the Good Message. He was punished because he had abused
the message of the Creator.

The White Race
(Hadihnyón:onh Denyonkhiyá:wek)

This is what the messengers said about the white race: [*]

We also hear your relations saying, "The white race is going
to exterminate you." We feel that Shongwayàdíhs:on is very
fond of His creation. He cares even more for the red people,
especially the ones that are poor. He protects the red race from
the white race. He has the power not to allow danger to prevail.

Education
(Adadrihonnyén:ni:)

The messengers said to Handsome Lake:

We feel that the white race will take away the culture,
traditions, and language of the red race.
  When your people's children become educated in the

---

[*] By the end of the American Revolutionary War the Iroquois saw that they were in a
position of great disadvantage: the white race had encircled them and were drawing the
lines ever tighter. Living as they were in the midst of a people against whom they had
fought not only in their own wars but also as allies of the British, it was no wonder they
were afraid. For they saw how all other native tribes had been swept away by the advance
of the invading race.
  The story of how they have preserved themselves through three centuries of contact
with an invading race that had little love for them and whose policy, like their own in
ancient times, was to assimilate or exterminate, is a marvel of history. They accomplished
what no other aboriginal race had done. Truly the Creator has cared for his red-skinned
people.

way of white people, they will no longer speak their own language and will not understand their own culture. Your people will suffer great misery and not be able to understand their elders anymore.

Your relations will appoint twelve children to be educated by the white race. They will select two children* from each of the Six Nations. We feel that when they become educated, not a single child will come back and stand at your side because they will no longer speak your language or have any knowledge of their culture.

Giving Thanks
(*Denyondennonhón:nyon:*)

The messengers said:

So now, according to the days the people have to live and rear their children, in the morning when they get up and when they are ready, they will come to the table to eat. It is the duty of the elderly person to thank the Creator for the food and for the fact that they are well and able to see the food prepared for them which will give them strength and power.

There is a reason for giving thanks: the Creator gave you the food you eat every day and you should be grateful. We

---

* Two children were selected from each tribe to receive the white race's education. The chiefs at the time believed that this education might benefit the native people.

By following the Good Message, the chiefs discovered that the education received from the white race robbed their children of their language and culture. They realized the importance of educating their own children.

should be thankful that He continues to give us the food we eat. Someday He may withdraw all sustenance of life.

A Widow Meets Another Man

The messengers said:

The way we see things, some women become widows. A woman had been a widow for some time. A man admired her and persuaded her to marry him.

So it truly happened that they came to live together. Now they had lived together only a short time when the man began to abuse the woman and her children.

This is what made the Creator sad.

If a man wishes to settle down with a widow, he must love her, treat her well, and love her children.

The message applies to both men and women.

Vanity (*Enaih agón:gweh*): A Proud Woman

This is what the messengers said about a woman who is proud of her appearance:

The way we see things, women like this are proud because they think they are better than others. Some women look down on others because they are not dressed properly; they are not satisfied with the way others look.

So this is what made Him sad, the One who created you. It would be the same if a person criticized Him for the way He looks, for He made humankind.

He intended people to have different features so that they could tell one from the other and not make a mistake. He created wildlife that roam the Earth. Many animals look alike — you could never say that the one you saw over there was the same one you saw yesterday. Animals know one another, but humankind has a problem seeing the difference.

Boasting
(*Gowihwagá:deh*)

This is what the messengers said about a man boasting of his strength and power:

We heard a man boasting. He said he was the strongest man.

He depended on his strength and power, and it is true that he was a strong man. This made him proud and brought him great sin here on Earth. He used his strength and power to abuse mankind.

The Creator intended that this kind of strength and power would be helpful to your relations. He made men different in strength and power. He intended that one man would be gifted with greater strength than another because some time in the future he would be needed to help others. The Creator did not want any person to abuse or hurt anyone. A person who kills another shall never see the land of the Creator. It is a sin to be proud of what you can do.

The strong man should give thanks to the Creator for giving him this kind of gift. He should say, "I thank You for giving me this strength and power to help others the way You intended me to do."

The Runner
(*Hayanó:weh*)

This is what the messengers said about a man who
is a fast runner:

The way we see things, some of your relations have been gifted more than others. Some people are gifted to be fast runners to convey an important message to others. But it seems that some are overly proud of what they are and also criticize and look down on other people within their nation.

Shongwayàdíhs:on did not intend it to be this way. When He made you, He thought that you would help others. He never thought His gifts would bring sin to your people. Your relations have been given these gifts and talents to help one another.

Lifestyle

This is what the messengers said about a native person who
builds a house the way a white man builds his house:

We think and feel there is no harm if your relations want to build a house the same way a white man builds his house. But tell your relations not to become overly proud by thinking they are better than another, if they build such a house.

Let it not bring sin to any of your relations. If he does not become overly proud, we feel that, when the man passes away, the house he built will stand and his family will benefit from it and enjoy it for much time to come.

Raising Livestock

*This is what the messengers said about the Ongwehónwe
raising livestock.*

We feel it would be all right if someone were to do the same
thing our white brothers do.

If anyone wishes to have domestic animals, it will benefit
his family for much time to come. He should treat his animals
well and respect them. He will do as our white brothers do.
They love and respect what they have. This is the reason the
Creator has given the white people all kinds of domestic
animals. He did not give them to the Ongwehónwe.

Cultivating the Land

*This is what the messengers said about how the Ongwehónwe
should cultivate the land:*

We feel there would not be any harm if your people want to
cultivate the land. Whenever a man works the land, his work
should be neat and well done. His work should be right so it
will produce things for his family to enjoy for much time to
come. It is important never to be too proud and for people
never to boast about what they can do. Avoiding this is a
good practice and will bring unity among all people.

*This is what the messengers said about a man going on a trip to
another village to visit his relations:*

The way we see things, a man had a family, and one day he
spoke to his wife about going on a trip to visit his relations
in another village. His wife agreed that he should go.

So truly when he visited his relations in the other village, he told the people there that he was not married. A woman believed him and became attracted to him.

In a short time his wife heard about what he was doing. Her mind was hurt and she was disappointed, so she went away and abandoned her family, leaving the children home alone. The children became poor. Both the man and the woman had neglected the children.

Small children can be hurt easily, as they are more sensitive than adults. Their spirits and minds do not stay here on Earth forever if they are unwanted. They think, "Our parents don't care for us. So it would be better if we were to go home to the spirit world."

So it happened that these children went home to the land of the Creator.

When the parents heard about this, they returned to their home and discovered that what they had heard was true: the house was vacant and the children had all died. They both wailed in grief. It seemed as if they did not realize what they had done.

We were anxious to see what happened. We were surprised. They came to live together again. So it seems they didn't like to have children. The children were only in the way.

Fidelity in Marriage

This part is what the messengers said about a man who goes on a hunting trip:

So truly a man and woman had a family. Now the man began thinking of going on a hunting trip, so he prepared himself and truly he went.

When he had hunted enough game, he thought of going home. He was fortunate in the game he killed, because it would be of great benefit to his family.

When he arrived at his village, he heard what his wife had done: while he was away she had been seeing another man.

So instead of staying home, he went to his relatives' place. When his wife heard that he had arrived at the village but that he had not come home, she went to where he was staying.

"Why did you go somewhere else?" she asked.

"The reason I did not go home is because of what you have done," he said.

She tried to deny it, but the way we see it, she truly had done what her husband claimed she had done.

This is a great matter of wrongdoing toward the Creator. He feels all these wrongdoings should cease.

This part is what the messengers said about a woman who admires another woman's husband:

Truly a married woman's mind was on someone else's husband. She was thinking how fortunate that woman was; she was provided for so well by her husband.

So the time came when she had a chance to talk to this man. She said to him, "Do you notice anything about your wife and my husband?" So it happened that this woman was able to break up the marriage and went to live with the man.

Shongwayàdíhs:on intended that some men would be better providers than other men. This is the way He intended things to be when He made humankind. Do not be jealous of others, because they have worked very hard for what they have. Do not be angry with yourself, just think how fortunate you are and be thankful for what you have. Hope for things to get better, and then leave matters in the hands of the Creator.

This part is what the messengers said about a man and woman who accuse one another because they cannot bear children:

The way we hear and see it, a man and his wife were talking, and the man was saying to his wife, "I think it is you who are unable to bear children."

And she replied, "It is you who are not able to give me children."

So it happened that they separated. They were separated only a short while before she met another man and became pregnant.

The day came when she gave birth to a child, whereupon she said to herself, "Maybe by now I could have had many more children."

We feel it is better to look for a mate who can bear children, but if neither the man nor the woman can have children, they may get along very well.

We can see each person's life and see into each person's mind. We see that a couple should never accuse each other for what they are. If they cannot have any children, then they should adopt a child. This is a good thing in the eyes of the Creator.

This is what the messengers said about a woman who does not bear children:

Now there are those who can never bear children. This is about such a woman who nevertheless wanted to have children. She could not bear children because when she was a small child, she had crawled on the floor and outside on the grass, where she ate grass and weeds that might have caused the harm.

This is what a person who cannot bear children should do: If she has a sister who has a large family, she may ask her sister to let her raise one of her children.

If the sister agrees, this is the way the woman should treat her adopted child. She is to rear the child in the way she would have if it had been her own. She is to speak to the child and tell her good things: the way her mind should be and how to be when she grows up.

When the child grows up, she will tell the child that she has done her duty and raised her. She will then say to the child, "Your mother lives over there. If you wish to go back and live with your mother, you are free to do so. But if you wish to stay here with me, you are also welcome to do so."

If any of your relations has raised three children, she may think, "I have done my duty."

If the woman abused the child while she was growing up, she did not gain anything, because she did not do the right thing. A person has done the right thing if she loves the child and repents of all her sins. If she has fulfilled the Good Message, then she has earned a reward from the Creator.

This part is what the messengers said about a man and wife who are always arguing:

Many of your relations have made a habit of arguing. If a man and wife start to argue as soon as they arise early in the morning, it will be the duty of the two elderly people who brought them together and confirmed the marriage to separate them.

We feel it would be better for the couple to separate, as

long as they do not have any children. We say this because otherwise they may accumulate much more sin.

This part is what the messengers said about a woman who is mean and cruel when she scolds her children:

Now the way we see it, a woman with a terrible temper may have a family. She will be too harsh when she scolds her children, punching and even kicking them.

We think and feel that she will injure the child because the child's body is so tender. The way Shongwayàdíhs:on intended it, water should be used to discipline a child. If the child disobeys her mother, then the mother should say, "I will throw water on your face." Or else she will say, "I am going to take you to the creek and dunk you in."

If this punishment does no good and the child does not give in, then she should use a red whip to punish her. The red whip should be about one summer old and a tobacco offering should be used when picking it.

After this, the child will notice and realize that her mother does mean what she says. Then the child will say, "I repent and will obey you."

Then the mother should stop punishing the child. If the mother continues to strike the child after the child has confessed, then it is a sin on the part of the mother.

This part is what the messengers said about a woman who takes her children's part:

Many times it happens in the way we see things among your neighbours that other children play around the house with a woman's children. Then suddenly one of her children comes running into the house crying.

The child says, "That child living in the next house hit me."

Then the mother will stop what she is doing and go to the neighbouring woman's house. She begins to say all sorts of bad things to her and makes things worse. Shortly afterwards, the children are playing together peacefully but there is still anger between the two women.

The woman believes what the child has said. Parents should never believe lies. They should teach their children to tell the truth first. Then they will be able to believe what they hear.

Medicine
(*Ononhkwá:thra*)

This is what the messengers said about the medicine spirits:

You don't realize that the Creator planted medicine for your relations to use. It grows all over the world. Do you hear the medicine spirits singing?

In their song, they are saying, "We are all over the land. We are ready to help if the people will come to us for help."

But now we hear your relations saying, "The medicine is not good."

The way we see your relations doing things, a woman gets ready, goes to the forest, and picks the medicine without an offering of natural tobacco or saying a word to the medicine.*

---

* When a person wishes to gather medicinal herbs, she goes into the woods where they grow and builds a small fire. When there is a quantity of glowing embers, she stands before it, and as she speaks, she casts, at intervals, a pinch of tobacco onto the coals. She speaks

The way Shongwayàdíhs:on intended, your relations will use the sacred native tobacco as an offering when gathering medicine. A person must offer tobacco and tell the medicine spirit what it is going to be used for and who is going to use it.

It is true that the medicine lives just like people. That is why it should be spoken to before it is picked.

This is what the messengers said about the medicine spirits who are listening while the Good Message is being preached:

Your relations do not realize that when the Good Message is preached, all the people should come and listen. For all the medicine spirits and for the supporters of life, come close and listen to the Good Message.

You should know that they listen and are faithful to the way the Creator intended. So truly these spirits do live just like people.

A person should go early in the morning to pick medicine while good spirits still exist. A person should not think of

---

to the spirits of the medicines, telling them that she desires their healing virtues to cure her people of their afflictions.

"You have said that you are ready to heal the earth," chants the gatherer of herbs, "so now I claim you for my medicine. Give me your healing virtues to purge and to cleanse and to cure. I will not destroy you but plant your seed that you may come again and yield fourfold more. Spirits of the herbs, I do not take your lives without purpose but to make you the agent of healing, for we are very sick. You have said that all the world might come to you, so I have come. I give you thanks for your benefits and thank the Creator for your gift."

When the last puff of tobacco smoke has risen, the gatherer of herbs begins his work. He digs the plant from the roots, and breaking off the seed stalks, drops the pods into the hole and gently covers them over with fertile leaf mould.

"The plant will come again," he says, "and I have not destroyed life but have helped it to multiply. So the plant is willing to lend me of its virtue."

picking medicine if they have just been to a funeral, and a person who has consumed alcohol should wait three days before picking medicine. A woman on her moon (menstrual period) should not pick medicine. Medicine is very sacred.

Gossip
(*Deyondrihwaén:donhkwa*)

*This is what the messengers said about a woman who
likes to gossip:*

The way we see things, a woman who lived in a neighbourhood decided to go and visit her neighbour. When she arrived at the neighbour's house, she talked about many things and the other woman listened to her.

Now the woman who was visiting said, "The reason I came here is to tell you something because I care for you. I was over at that woman's house and I was really surprised at the things she said about you. This is the main reason that I came here to see you."

Then the woman of the house began to say many things and they both criticized the woman at the other house.

Now it seems as if the woman was in a hurry to leave and go home, but instead of going straight home she went directly to where the other woman lived. She did the same thing again, talking about the other things first for a short while and then saying the things she really wanted to say.

She began by saying, "I just came from that woman's house. She said many bad things about you and that is the reason I came here to tell you because I care a lot for you."

All the things that happened were the visiting woman's

fault. Evil came between all these women. This one woman made up the stories to stir up bad feelings between the two other women.

If someone has this habit, we call that woman a gossiper. She made up all kinds of lies just to create bad feelings between others. When your relations hear our message, they will repent of this evil practice and make it everlasting as long as they live here on Earth.

This is how things should be when a person has a visitor:

The way the Creator intended it, they should speak only of good things that will not hurt anyone's feelings. The visitor should offer to help the other woman with her work, as the woman may be harvesting what she planted.

So as they work, everything will be peaceful. By the time they depart, everything will be well and good. This is the way the Creator would like things to be.

Selfishness
(*Gosgenhá:seh*)

This is what the messengers said about a woman who was a very selfish person:

The way we see things, a person had a family, the children were playing outside, and the mother was preparing food for them to eat. She had already set the food on the table when suddenly the children noticed a woman coming towards the house. One of the children went in and told their mother.

Then the woman took all the food off the table and put

it away. She didn't have much time, but managed to put all the food away by the time the woman arrived. The woman stayed only a short time, because she understood everything and noticed that the woman disapproved of her visit.

As soon as the visitor left, the woman placed the food back on the table.

So now you will relate this message to your relations: When they hear of these wrongdoings, they will repent of all their sins for as long as they live here on Earth.

Generosity
(*Godennidén: on*)

This is what the messengers said about a woman who is a generous person:

Sometimes you may have visitors. You will always offer food to them, because that is the way He intended it to be. The woman of the house should always offer a meal to her visitors.

It may happen that some children will visit. If she hears them playing near her house, she should invite them to come in and offer them food to eat, as one may be very poor and hungry.

Offering food to children is a great thing to do for the Creator. If someone visits and does not accept a meal that is offered to them, this is wrong. The way He intended it, a person should sit down and join them and have something anyway. That is the right way. If the visitor does not accept a meal, then the person offering it may feel that her food is not good enough, and this could bring disappointment to the woman of the house.

He who made you says that if you have just finished a meal before arriving at the person's house and the woman of the house offers a meal, you should accept the offer. You will give thanks for the offering by saying, "I thank you for offering a meal. Don't feel bad but I ate before leaving home."

So this is the way the Creator intended things to be when a person visits another person.

Old Age
(*Enyonhtgénhjihs*)

This is what the messengers said about people who have reached old age:

The way we see things, when a relation of yours reaches old age, she becomes helpless in many ways: she is neglected; her family do not respect her; they talk about her in low voices. She is feeble and old and she cannot help herself. She has lost her sight and cannot hear very well. She goes back into her childhood ways again.

It is wrong in the eyes of the Creator and it makes Him sad when you neglect the elderly. This becomes a great sin of the people on Earth.

This is what the messengers said about a family that supports and assists the elderly:

The way the Creator ordained things, people should live to reach old age. However, when they reach old age, they lose their strength, become disabled, and even lose their sight. So now it is the duty of the younger one, one who has strength and health, to support the elderly person.

She will wash her face, comb her hair, and bathe her. She

will prepare food for her and feed her because she is unable to help herself. She will treat the elderly person in the same way that she would treat an infant child.

Parents should respect the elderly in every way. This is the way children will also learn how to respect elderly people.

The time has come as predicted by the elders when young people no longer respect the elderly. This is why the elderly are placed in old age homes today.

A person should always be good and polite to the elderly. They should provide everything the elderly person needs. Then they will earn a reward from the Creator.

Traditional Clothing
(*Ahgwennyaón:weh*)

This is what the messenger said about the traditional clothes that
are to be worn at certain times:

There will be a time when the traditions and customs of the
clothing you wear will change. However, your people should
wear traditional clothes at certain times when needed.

A person who wears his traditional clothes should walk
around the outside of the house and think how fortunate he
is because of his health and ability to attend ceremonies. He
should say, "I thank the Creator for giving me this day and
that I am still alive."

So that is the reason your relations should be prepared
and have their traditional clothes ready to wear at certain
times, including the day they pass away.

Medicine for Three Sisters
(*Tyonnhé:gonh Onennonhgwá:thra*)

This is what the messengers said about what will happen if the
corn does not grow again:

The Creator has given you corn for food to live on. Some
day the corn may not grow, or it may begin to grow but look
sickly. So your relations must know there is medicine for
them, which should be gathered just before planting.

The medicine is called *gosdisdén:ni,* and it is gathered
fresh from the forest. The seed corn should be soaked in this

solution before planting so that it will be free from disease and will grow well.

So this is the kind of medicine He has planted for your relations to use. He has given us medicine to cure disease, and He has given the corn, beans, and squash a medicine because they have a living spirit.[*]

---

* Corn, beans, and squash were grown together and were known as the Three Sisters, or the supporters of life.

The ceremony of invoking the Creator over the hills of corn was an old one, and like many other old customs was endorsed by Handsome Lake. This custom is still continued among some of the Iroquois. When the leaf of hickory is the size of a squirrel's ear, the planting season has come.

Years ago, the people always soaked the seeds for two days in a container before planting.

When planting is finished, the whole family will go to the field dressed in their traditional clothes. They will all stand in the middle of the cornfield, and the elder will speak on behalf of his family. He will say, "We hope everything is well and good so we may see the Three Sisters ripen again, which will be our food." This is what the messengers said.

Extinction of Species
(*Wadókdahne Gadí:nyo:*)

This is what the messengers said about the new species the Creator will bring to the native people when the deer becomes extinct:

This is the way we see things among your relations: If they are able to fulfill the Good Message, the Creator will create a new species of deer (male and female).* They will be seen one day. Your people will say, "They are over there." There will be two. The male deer will be white-spotted and the female deer will be white-striped over her back.

When this pair of deer is seen, your relations are not to kill them, so they may populate.

Truly it did happen. A time came when the people saw

The medicine, *gosdisdén:ni*, used for the plant's seeds, is known as phragmites in English. Another medicine, *osa'gén:dah* (*Hystrix patula*), or bottle-brush grass, was also used at times. The roots of this plant were boiled and then put into the container of seeds.

* These deer are the sacred creations of the Creator and as such, no one is permitted to see them, though a few of the people have at certain seasons seen them fleeing in the darkness, so as not to be discovered. It was said that these deer were killed by a jealous rival of Handsome Lake while he was still living, thus defying the new command.

them. And a man who did not respect the rules of the Creator destroyed the deer.

Extended Life

This is what the messengers said about life being extended by the Creator if the Good Message is fulfilled:

The way the Creator intended it, if your relations fulfill the Good Message, the Creator will extend the life of Mother Earth for another three generations. All this will happen if your relations make an effort to honour the Good Message and repent of all their sins.

Faithkeepers
(*Honadríhont*)

This part is about the faithkeepers who go hunting for the Great Ceremony.[*]

The messengers said, "A group of faithkeepers will go out hunting and you will watch. If they are able to fell thirty deer, you will know that your relations have fulfilled their duty according to the Good Message.

Handsome Lake said, "I watched and truly they went hunting the deer. They killed twenty-eight deer."

So they were short two to make it thirty, the set number they were to kill. Thus, they were not able to fulfill the Good Message.

---

[*] The Great Ceremony refers to the Midwinter Ceremony, a celebration expressing gratitude for the completion of the cycle of the year.

The messengers said that the Creator ordained that there will always be faithkeepers.

He who made you intended there would be faithkeepers (men and women).

The way He intended it, the faithkeepers will set the time for and conduct the four sacred ceremonies. So if someone has fulfilled the Good Message and has always been faithful and done the right thing, such a person is very fortunate and has earned a reward from the Creator when she or he passes away on Earth.

The Four Ceremonies (*Géih Niyowihwá:ge:*)

This is what the messengers said about the four ceremonies the Creator has sanctioned:

Now hear these words about the four ceremonies He gave you that He sanctioned from His land in the spirit world.

The first thing your relations will do is to have the children's special day, where you will honour the children and where the infants will be given names.

The first dance is the Great Feather Dance and the second dance is the Skin Dance, or Drum Dance. When the ceremony begins, we give thanks and honour the four messengers.

The third ceremony is a dance to give thanks to Him who made you, a dance in honour of the Creator. The Great Feather Dance (*Ganonnyowá:nenh Ostowahgó:wa*) is a great event, including the personal ceremonial chant (*adón:wah*), reciting what the Creator has provided for the people.

In the fourth great event, you will honour the Creator with the Great Peach Stone and Bowl Game, which you will play to entertain the Creator. There will also be a special ceremony for the supporters of life: corn, beans, and squash (the Three Sisters — *tyonnhé:gonh*).

◈

THE CHILDREN'S SPECIAL DAY

The First Ceremony: The Great Feather Dance (*Ganonnyowá:nenh Ostowahgv:wa*)

Everyone should repent of their sins before the ceremonies begin, because that is the way the Creator intended things to be, for everyone should be clean and pure before beginning the ceremonies. You will comfort and encourage the infant children because they have no sin and the Creator is very fond of the tiny ones.

It is important that your relations should start the ceremony early in the morning. Before the ceremony begins, your relations will prepare a kettle of corn soup to honour the little children.

There will come a day when a shortage of wild game will occur. Animals will become extinct and this is beyond your control. In the meantime, however, the Creator has sanctioned the domestic animal to be used for feasting and thanksgiving. The meat is added to flavour the soup.

The Great Feather Dance is the first thanksgiving ceremony.

The Second Ceremony:
The Skin Dance
(*Ganéhon:*)

This part is what the messengers said about the Skin Dance.

The way we see things, when the Skin Dance begins, everyone will take part in the dancing. The dancing will stop at certain times, and a man will give thanks on behalf of the people.

One man spoke on his own behalf about how many people he had scalped, the way he did it in his early days when charms and warpaint were used for added strength and power. Now this wrongdoing must cease.

(This was the custom in the days before Handsome Lake. The Three Celestial Beings told the prophet that this practice of scalping, charms, and warpaint must stop.)

The messengers said, "Only one person will be appointed as speaker to speak on behalf of the people. He will talk about the contents of Mother Earth and what the Creator has given you and will end his speech where the Creator dwells. This is the way it will be from now on."

The Third Ceremony:
Honouring the Creator
(*Hodisgenengé:da Dehonwanonhonyónhá*)

This is how the messengers said the Creator is to be honoured:

So now when you are ready to honour and give thanks to the Creator, the first ceremony you will perform is the Great Feather Dance. The second ceremony is performed by men to give thanks to the Creator and to celebrate their existence on this Earth through the thanksgiving chant (*adón:wah*).

The faithkeepers will go out and notify the people in the community. They will say, "It is the time for you to come and honour the Creator with the ceremonies He has given you."

The way we see things, your relations don't realize what is happening on Earth. The Evil Spirit and his helpers are also busy informing the people in the community. The Evil Spirit's helpers are saying, "You do not have to go to the Longhouse for the ceremonies. You have many other things to do which would benefit you more." The Evil Spirit keeps talking and tries to persuade your relations not to go to the Longhouse. So that is the way it is when the Evil Spirit knows there is a ceremony to take place at the Longhouse when your relations are about to honour the Creator.

A person prepares to go to the Longhouse. While she is walking along, the Evil Spirit is following her and tries to persuade her to turn around and go home. The Evil Spirit does not give up hope as he follows.

When she approaches the Longhouse, he says, "You have arrived at the Longhouse. Now you should only stand outside. That is good enough. You don't have to go inside. You can just sit here outside the Longhouse." The woman goes inside the Longhouse, but the Evil Spirit still does not give up hope, and he is walking alongside her. Again, he says to her, "Now you have arrived, that is good enough, just sit and watch the way things go on."

So the Evil Spirit is successful, convincing her to sit and look on and not to participate in the ceremony. So this is what happens to your relations on Earth.

Now we will talk about a person who is not able to participate because they are sick and cannot get around very well.

The way the Creator intended it, such a person should

take part in the ceremonial dances and go around three times, and they will have done their duty and will thank the Creator for being able to attend the ceremonies.

Now the infant children will wish that they were able to join in the dances to thank the Creator. They way He intended it, the infants should also participate because they know there is a ceremony. They also know that the ceremonies go on in the land of the Creator where they came from. They know this because they have no sin.

The Fourth Ceremony:
The Peach Stone and Bowl Game
(*Gayendowá:nen*)

This is what the messengers said about the Great Betting Day when the Peach Stone and Bowl Game* is played:

The fourth great ceremony He gave you is called the Great Betting Game (or the Peach Stone and Bowl Game), in which you are to honour Him.

---

*   In 1898 archaeologist David Boyle of Toronto observed and recorded the playing of the Peach Stone and Bowl Game. He wrote in an archaeological report: "It is only in connection with the midwinter and fall festivals that the practice of public offerings is permitted. On these occasions there is high revelry.

"All the goods collected as stakes by six men are piled in one or two heaps, the articles being tied or pinned in pairs with some regard to respective values or uses. Thus, there may be two silk neckties, two pairs of moccasins, two shawls, or two strings of *otgo:a* (wampum), which is regarded as taking first place at such times.

"The old men of the nation appoint two men, one from each side of the Longhouse, to call out the male players, and, similarly, two women for a like purpose.

"A blanket is spread on the floor of the Longhouse, and in the middle of this sheet rests the wooden bowl, about 14 or 16 inches across the center and 4 to 5 inches deep, containing six peach stones rubbed down to smooth surfaces and blackened on one side. Near the south edge of the blanket is placed a vessel containing 100 beans, from which stock seven are taken by each of the men who act as callers. All players are sitting east and west of one another.

You will entertain and honour Him by loud cheers when you play this game. You will honour Him by betting the most valuable and precious things you have. You will thank Him with the turtle rattle, lacrosse stick, or ceremonial clothing.

If a person loses the game, losing some things they betted to the winners of the game, this person must know that they will see their possessions in the spirit world. They will thereby have fulfilled the Good Message and repented of all their sins.

Corn, Beans, Squash
(Onénhen, Osahé:da, Ohnyónhsah)

This is what the messengers said about the supporters of life, the Three Sisters (tyonnhé:gonh): *

The way we see things, when you honour the supporters of life (the corn, bean, and squash spirits), they want to be a

---

"The first player takes the bowl by the edge with both hands and after a few preliminary shakes in midair he strikes the bottom sharply on the floor, when the peach stones rebound and fall back within the dish.

"Winning throws are of four kinds: All white, all black, one white, or one black. All black or white means that the woman representing the winner receives from him who represents the loser 5 beans, but when only one white or one black stone shows face up, 1 bean is the gain. If, however, any player makes three successive casts, winning 5 each time, he is allowed 15 additional beans, and similarly, after 3 successive casts winning 1 each, he is allowed 3 more beans.

"As long as a player makes winning throws he keeps his place, which when he leaves is immediately taken by another — man or woman. In this way the game is continued until one side wins all the beans, and this may require only an hour or two, or it may take two to three days."

* The reason for having the supporters of life in the ceremony is to show them gratitude. One time when Handsome Lake went for a walk in his garden to see the Three Sisters, he noticed a corn leaf. This corn leaf touched his shoulder and the corn spirit spoke to him.

part of the ceremonies, as they play a great role every day in
your lives.

The corn, bean, and squash spirits wish to be honoured
in the same way that you honour the Creator when there is
a ceremony for Him.

She said, "We are very sad that your people do not give thanks when a ceremony is taking
place. We would like to be a part of the ceremony because we are the supporters of life
for all people. Maybe we should leave with you and go back to the spirit world."

Handsome Lake replied, "I am not the one to say that you are to leave the Earth. The
Creator will be the one to call you when the time comes. What I will do to encourage you
is to honour all of you at the ceremonies."

The Strawberry Ceremony
(*Hennadahyaó:he:s Jihsón:da:*)

This is what the messengers said about the Early Wild
Strawberry Ceremony:

The Creator did something great for your relations when He planted the early berries, which you call strawberries. When the time of season has arrived that the berries are first seen, the faithkeepers will discuss the date to be set for the ceremony.

The people will assemble in the Longhouse and give thanks, because the time has come again when we see the Earth bear fruit. This is what the Creator planted on Earth for you to use.

If it should happen in the future that the strawberry plants will not bear fruit, then you should pick (or gather) only the red leaves and these should be made into a drink.

The ceremony should begin early in the morning and be completed by noontime. The strawberry drink should be served to everyone. Each person should offer thanks before drinking it and be grateful for all things.

Two people, ones who do not have any sin, will be appointed to serve the drink. You will honour the strawberry spirit and the Creator in the Great Feather Dance. During intermission, when the first set of dancing stops, then the drink will be served to the audience. Everyone should give a short speech of thanks before drinking it. All the people and the children who are assembled will give thanks to the Creator.

The Early String Bean Ceremony
(*Hennadesahedaó:he:s*)

This is what the messengers said about the
*Early String Bean Ceremony:**

We feel it is a great thing that the Creator planted the string beans for your relations to use. There is a certain time in the season when the first vegetables grow — they are called string beans. So the way He intended, when you see the beans grow and bear beans, that is the time the faithkeepers should hold the ceremony for giving thanks.

This ceremony should start early in the morning when your relations honour the spirit of the bean and the Creator in the Great Feather Dance.

The Bean Ceremony is held to give gratitude to Mother Earth and all the supernatural beings and the Creator for letting the Earth people see their sustenance grow again.

The Midwinter Ceremony
(*Géih Niyowihwá:ge Tshadegohsráhen*)

*This is what the messengers said about the Midwinter Ceremony:***

The great ceremonies uphold the customs of the native people.
When certain individuals belong to totem societies, they

---

*   The Bean Ceremony is the first ceremony celebrating the Three Sisters. People bring their green beans to cook for the ceremony, then the beans are served and shared by all after the ceremony. This is a time of thankfulness by all.

**   The Midwinter Ceremony is one of the longest ceremonies of the whole cycle. In will honour the totem animals and hold pass dance songs to confirm their connection with the guardian totem. This is to be done in their own homes.

Your relations will hold this ceremony in the month of December, five sleeps after the new moon.

A Man Who Constantly Desires Women

This is what the messengers said about a man who constantly desires to have new experiences with more and more women:

Many of your relations have these desires, and it seems your people don't have any respect for one another, or for mar-

---

olden times, people made new fires on the morning of the day the ceremony began. Two chiefs would go around the village and stir the ashes in the people's longhouse fires. This was seen as doing away with old fires and making new fires, completing the cycle once again.

Early in the month of October, the men go out to hunt the deer and return in December for the Midwinter Ceremony. The people honour the animals at this time for giving their lives for the ceremony.

The new cycle starts at the time of the maple syrup harvest (*hennadrennawendaó : he :s*), when Mother Earth starts her new cycle again.

Another means of preparing for a new cycle was purification. The herb used most extensively by the Iroquois for "purification" was red willow, the bark of which was used both as an emetic and as a purgative. For an emetic, the bark was peeled upward and for a purgative, it was peeled downward.

Early in the spring during the spell of warm days, the people would take their kettles, jars of soup, and deerskins, and go alone into the woods for their ceremony of purification. Here they would scrape the bark. The drink was taken in large quantities and then the person would sit wrapped in his deerskin to await the results.

From sunrise to sunset the drink would be taken until the alimentary tract was completely emptied. Toward sundown a little soup would be sipped to ward off excessive weakness, and for strength to return home. Often on the next morning sweat baths were taken, and then solid food was eaten. This process was thought to purify the body and without doubt did much to do so. Besides customary spring purification, others were sometimes ordered for disease and for preparations for ordeals, tests, and ceremonial purposes. The process was repeated in the autumn.

riage. There are men who constantly desire new experiences.

Some men would like to know more and more young women and there will never be an end to this habit.

If someone hearing this message has these desires, he will repent at once and make his repentance everlasting as long as he lives on Earth.

Medicine People
(*Dehayàdowéh:tha*)

This part is about certain people who have the power to judge diseases and recommend cures:

The messengers said to Handsome Lake, "You have been given the power to judge diseases and recommend cures. When the time comes for you to exercise your power, we will tell you when you are to begin."

In a few days Handsome Lake's brother, Cornplanter (Gáyentwágeh), arrived at the prophet's house. Cornplanter wanted his brother to judge his daughter's disease. But the prophet did not answer Cornplanter's question.

Only a few days later, Cornplanter came again and talked about the same thing, but this time he brought some sacred tobacco with him. Again our great leader did not answer his question.

Cornplanter became angry at his brother and said many harsh words to him. Cornplanter said to him, "The things you preach cannot be true; that is why you do not want to help me." Again our leader said nothing.

Cornplanter came three times to see him. Each time he talked about the same thing. The third time the great leader answered his question. He said, "I will judge it even though I was not told to do so yet."

He began to judge it and he saw the problem (the songs of all sacred societies and social dances were being abandoned). In judging, he saw that many people in the village were sick in bed.

So this is what happened at that time. The people recognized that the social songs and the songs of the totem societies had been abandoned. They began to practise them again at the time when the prophecy was new. The people were very faithful to the societies to which they belonged.

The messengers arose again and said, "This is what happened. You judged the disease but we did not give you the right to start to exercise your power. We were to say when you would begin and you were aware of what we said. You would have been able to see far down into the Earth's surface, as far down as a tree's longest root, if you had waited.

"We feel that there will be many people who will be judging diseases in the future. It will not be good. It will be the work of the Evil Spirit.

"You will also relate this message to your relations. The songs and dances are being continued among the people that belong to certain societies. This is the way it shall be if anyone wishes to hold the songs and dances: Food is to be prepared for the feast and only food is to be served.

"Now this wrongdoing of serving strong drinks must stop and cease forever when holding these dances. Everyone should be sober whenever holding feasts and dances."

Cornplanter again tried to bring his brother into disfavour with the Four Messengers by forcing him to exercise his powers prematurely. For this reason the followers of Handsome Lake to this day regard Cornplanter as a malicious character who always tries to upset the *Gaiwí:yo*, or Good Message.

Failure to Repent
(*Adathrewáh:don:*)

This part is about three people who did not confess or repent at the time when the prophecy was new:

So this is what happened when the prophecy was new, when the people heard the Good Message from the Creator. The chiefs in those days tried to persuade the people to repent of their sins but three people did not honour the Good Message and did not repent.

So the great leaders and chiefs decided what they should do for those who failed to honour the Good Message and would not repent before they passed away on Earth.

"Let us cast them into the water after they pass away because they are so wicked and the Creator does not care for them anymore."

So when the messengers arose and appeared before our great leader, the chiefs had already decided what they would do. But the messengers said to Handsome Lake:

"Tell your people not to do what your leaders have agreed upon. He never intended it to be that way. He did not give you the right to judge and punish mankind. There is a place where a person will be punished if he or she disobeys the teaching and fails to fulfill the Good Message."

The Children
(*Hadiksàshón:a*)

This part is about the children and Handsome Lake:

Our leader was given comfort and courage by the children. The messengers said to our great leader, "We know what you are thinking about. You feel that the people have neglected you and what you talked about. So this is what your relations will do. You will be given courage by the children."

Truly it was done, and the children were invited to assemble in the Longhouse.

The leaders had selected two boys to talk to him and give him courage. So this is what our great leader used to say. The two boys were not able to say a word to him. They only broke out in tears and started to cry. So then they appointed another boy. The boy they appointed seemed as if he was bold and had a strong mind.

Truly he was able to speak a few words. He said to the prophet, "Thank you. Have courage, Grandpa." That was all he was able to say to our great leader.

Faith
(*Áhsen Niyowihwá:ge*)

The messengers told Handsome Lake to call his people to a meeting at the Longhouse. At that time he was to address people who were experiencing problems in accepting the Good Message he was preaching. They told him to walk around the house speaking first to one, then to another.

The messengers said, "You are to say, 'Is there anyone here who would like me to convince them to accept this belief? If so, speak up now, for the time to repent is now.'

"You will also say, 'Is there anyone here who would like to sit and stare at one spot? That is what the four men who were unrepentant did. Perhaps there are still those who have not listened but only sat and stared. If so, speak up now, for the time to repent is soon.'

"You will also ask if anyone likes to run through the woods. These are people who sin and have lost their way. They do not come to the Longhouse. You will say, 'If there are any among you who are lost in this way, speak up now because soon it may be too late.'

"You will ask of all if there is anyone who likes to go visiting. Visitors are those who go from Longhouse to church and back again. They change their beliefs and do not commit themselves to their traditional ceremonies. You will say, 'If there is anyone who likes to visit, speak up now, for the time will soon come to make a choice.'"

The Effects of Alcohol
(*Ohné:gah*)

This is what the messengers said about a test between strong drinks and food: *

The people say that there is nothing wrong with drinking because it is made from fermented food. So this is the

---

* It is related that at one period whiskey had so debauched the natives that their sacred ceremonies, like those of the early Christians at Corinth, were made the excuses of the grossest licentiousness and drunken revelry. Whiskey had entirely supplanted the feast foods.

reason we thought your relations should try it by dividing the people into two groups. Food will be served at one end and strong drinks will be served at the other end.

They will sit in two groups at each end and start at the same time. At one end they will start to eat and at the other end they will start to drink.

So we feel there will be a dead person at the end where the strong drinks were served by the time everyone is finished.

This will be a test for your people to see which will benefit mankind — food or alcohol.

Three Stages

Handsome Lake moved to Cold Spring, New York, and stayed there for two years, continuing his duty and teaching the Good Message. At this time he had a revelation. His work would be completed when he had walked his journey three times. This is what the messengers said: "At the third stage, you will think you have entered eternity in the spirit world.

"You will have three sacred personal songs. So this is the way it will be. You must consider the right way and decide when you will sing your song.

"All the people will be given a song to sing when they leave Mother Earth and take the path to the spirit world. They will not know their song until they are ready to leave Mother Earth."

Punishment for Mind Control
(Onónhwet)

This part is about two women who committed a crime while Handsome Lake was still living at Cold Spring.

The chiefs in those days had a meeting and decided to punish the two women (a mother and daughter) because they had committed a crime. They had administered witch powder* to a man, and he had lost his mind and later died.

---

* Witch powders were used for various purposes but generally as poisons or love charms to control a person's mind.

So our great leader heard what the chiefs decided and agreed to punish them by whipping them. Each chief would give one lash to each of the two women. So the two women hardly survived the punishment they received.

So when the three messengers rose again, this was the first matter they mentioned to our great leader. They said, "You heard everything when the chiefs made their decision and you did not say anything about it."

Our great leader replied, "The reason I did not say a word about it was because I thought the women might live and survive."

The messengers said, "The Creator did not intend that you would punish your people. So now this will stop and cease forever. There is a place where a person will go and be punished if he disobeys the words of the Creator."

The Power to Judge Diseases (*Dehayàdowéh: Tha:k*)

It is true that our great leader was given power to judge disease. While our great leader was still living at the village of Cold Spring, a father and son arrived from the village of Cattaraugus, New York, on their way to hunt deer. They stayed until morning and then continued on their journey.

After only a short time the boy came back. He said, "Has anyone seen my father? I think he must be lost. Did he come back this way?"

The chiefs became suspicious about what the boy said. They said, "This cannot be true, what he has said."

The chiefs wanted to have the matter examined. They

pleaded with our great leader to exercise his powers to judge this matter. So he did judge it.

Our leader said, "I will practise it even though I was not given the word from the messengers. You will place these items on the floor: a bullet, knife, and hatchet."

Our great leader said, "Now you shall watch closely which one moves. Then you will think that is the one that did it."

They watched and saw the bullet move. The bullet is the one that had killed the man. The boy had shot his father.

Then our great leader said, "I understand quite clearly what I saw in my vision. There is a hill over there, and around the middle of that hill, there is a huge tree with its large branch broken off touching the ground. There is a crotch at the foot of the large branch, and his fody is lying there in the middle of it."

So then the men set out to look for the body and truly that is where they found the body and there was a bullet hole in his chest. So this proved that the son had shot his father. It also showed the people that the prophet had the power to judge.

A Dead Man's Chest
(Tgaahsaní:yonht Tshenhónweh Dedyothahó:gen)

The messengers said to Handsome Lake, "Look and watch closely." They pointed out a certain spot.

Handsome Lake saw something that looked like a man's chest floating in the air from a branch, with a hole in the middle of the chest. It seemed someone had shot it.

So the messengers said to him, "We hung it there because

it is an important matter that happened in the past. We have caused this dreadful thing to be done so that when the murderer approaches, he will be confronted with his evil. The son who killed his father will see the work of his hand when he comes this way.

Stealing
(*Enénhsgwas*)

This is what the messengers said to Handsome Lake about a
*woman tempted by someone else's vegetable garden:**

You shall relate this message to your relations. Whenever someone sees fresh green vegetables growing in someone's garden that she would like to have, then she will go to the woman's house and take something to trade.

She will say, "I saw something in your garden that I would like to have, so I brought this for trade."

It will then be up to the owner of the garden to accept the item for trade or to just let the woman have the vegetables without accepting any trade or charge. The gardener should not set a price but should give the woman whatever she wants from the garden. If she accepts as a trade whatever the woman brought with her, she should give her more from the garden than the woman wanted.

So this is the way we see things.

---

* One of the old methods of gardening was to clear a small plot in the forest or in a meadow. The name and totem of the owner of the garden was painted on the longhouse, and the clan totem gave permission to anyone who asked or needed to take what they wished from the garden for trade or as a gift. These gardens in the forests were often a temptation, as the prophet related in his message to the people.

Sometimes the woman takes something without asking and feeds her children these things that she has stolen. That is wrongdoing. It is like feeding the children fire, even though the children are contented, not knowing that their mother had stolen the things she gave them.

Handsome Lake Visits Philadelphia

When the Good Message was new, the people first heard it preached at a place called Burnt House (Dyononhsadé:genh) in Cornplanter's village, but in 1802 Handsome Lake and his followers went to visit President Thomas Jefferson

("The-town-destroyer") in Philadelphia to talk about the Good Message. Handsome Lake was also accompanied by the chiefs when he made this long journey.

Our leader spent three days there, talking about the Good Message. The president of the Thirteen Colonies confirmed the Good Message and said to our leader, "Be stingy with your belief. It is good for your people — preach it to your children and continue to have faith in your belief."

President Jefferson had Secretary of War and General Henry Dearborn write a letter commending the teachings of Handsome Lake. He stated, "Brothers — The President is pleased to see you all in good health, after so long a journey, and rejoices in his heart that one of your own people has been employed to make you sober, and of good mind. He is well disposed to give you good advice, and to set before you good examples.

"Brothers — If all the red people follow the advice of your friend and teacher, Handsome Lake, and in future will be sober, honest, industrious, and good, there can be no doubt but the Great Spirit will take care of you and make you happy."

Predictions

This is what the messengers said about a time when the chiefs would only quarrel when they held their councils:[*]

There will be a time when your relations will see this happen: the chiefs will hold councils, but they will only quarrel among themselves.

---

[*] Handsome Lake talked about the principles of the Code. He also said, "The Great Law talks of chiefs cultivating good minds among everybody and having respect for each other. This is the only way unity can continue to exist."

It is predicted that the chiefs will throw ashes at one another, which means that they will only argue among themselves. So whenever this happens, you will feel the time is getting near. Something is going to happen to Mother Earth.

The way we think and feel, this is going to happen to your relations sometime in the future. Your relations will no longer wish to hear or honour the Good Message.

This prediction is about an object with wheels on it with no horse pulling it. The messengers said:

We think and feel that some day this is going to happen: Your people will see something and it will have wheels and there will be nothing pulling it and it will be moving along by itself and it will take many lives. Then your people will think the time is getting near.

This prediction is about an old woman who will bear a child. The messengers said:

An old woman who used to bear children will again bear a child, although she had not been with child since she was young.

Then your people will think the time is getting near.

This prediction is about a little girl who will bear a child. The messengers said:

Some day in the near future you and your people will see a little girl bear a child, even though she is too young to bear a child.

So we feel when this happens it will be a surprise to your relations. Then you will think that the time is getting near.

This is what the messengers predicted about assembling in the Longhouse for the ceremonies:

We think and feel that in the future your relations shall see the people assemble to give thanks to the Creator but they will not be able to carry out the ceremony and will just disperse.

This is what the messengers predicted about witchcraft (góhtgonh):

We think and feel that it will happen that a woman will be seen performing witchcraft in the daylight. There will be no secrets about it anymore.

She will also tell others about this and there will be no fear of telling that she has administered witch-powdered roots and herbs that have destroyed many lives.

Your relations will notice that there will be some kind of animal seen running about in the daylight. When this happens, your relations will think that the time is getting near, the end of Mother Earth.

The messengers predicted an epidemic — an unknown disease that would kill many people.

If your relations do not fulfill the Good Message, many people will face hardships and will suffer this disease.

This is what the messengers predicted about the elders and the small children returning to the land of the Creator.

We think and feel it is going to happen when the end is near that the small children who have no sin will go home to the land of the Creator. The elderly people will go to sleep and will not wake up again, and that is the last.

A child may go outside and never return, and the mother will go out to look for her and only her tracks will be seen. The child's footprints will seem to have faded away.

The child will be picked up by the Four Celestial Beings.

The people who have fulfilled the Good Message will see the land of the Creator. The children who have no sin will also see the land of the Creator.

The reason this will happen is that the Creator does not want anyone who has repented to see what will happen when Mother Earth will come to an end.

We think and feel this is going to happen because there will be too many evil things that will continue among your people. The people are evil and sinful — some even go so far as to do evil things in their own houses. Their own family will be wicked and will quarrel among themselves.

This is what the messengers said to the prophet:

When the time comes, your relations will not honour the Good Message. Now you must relate this to your relations. This is what will happen if your people fail to fulfill and honour the Good Message. The Creator will withdraw all sustenance of life. The people who fail to repent will suffer hardships. When this happens, there will be many elderly people and many children in grief and sorrow because there will be no food to be found. An elderly person will go out to look for food, but she will return with nothing.

The messengers predicted that the Creator will stop the motion of the sun.

When the motion of the sun stops, there will be much greater darkness than usual. The creatures will be released from the underground. Your relations will see many powerful creatures that they have never seen before, and many people will be destroyed by them. The only time it will get bright again is when Mother Earth starts to burn. Not a single person will escape from the fire on Earth when the time comes. No one will be able to survive when this happens to Mother Earth. Those who do not repent or reform will remain on Earth and will see this happen.

The Sky-Road

This part is about the messengers taking Handsome Lake to the sky-road to view his world below and see the future:

Handsome Lake said, "I never thought that the sun was that high above the Earth as we walked along the path."

As they proceeded on their journey, it seemed they were not walking the right way. It seemed something was pushing them with force. So then the messengers said, "Here we will tarry a while."

Then the messengers said to him, "What did you notice while we were walking?"

He replied, "I felt I could run for a long distance if a message needed to be delivered."

This is how our great leader used to tell it.

A Vision
(*Ahsen Nigendyogwá:eg:*)

This part is about the three groups of people:

The messengers said again to our great leader, "You will look back on Earth."

So truly he did look and saw three different sizes of

groups. The first group was small, with only a few people. The second group of people was about medium-sized. The third group of people was a larger group.

They said to him, "What did you observe? How did it look to you?"

He said, "I saw people standing there in three groups. There were also three different-sized groups of people: small, medium, and large."

Then the messengers said, "It is true the way you understood and observed what you saw. The people you saw were grouped according to believers of the Good Message. The largest group are the unbelievers. The second-largest group are the ones who have some belief. The smallest group are those who truly believe in the Good Message and live according to their responsibilities."

Greed
(*Goskenhá:seh Agongweh Egówanen*)

This part is about a greedy and selfish person:

The messengers said to Handsome Lake, "Look back down on Earth."

So he did, and they said to him, "What do you see and observe?"

He said, "I see a woman. She is sitting on the ground. She is a very big woman. She is grasping all the things she can reach and putting the things beside her."

Then they said, "You are right in the way you have observed what you saw. You have seen what we call a very greedy and selfish person. She will always be that way as long as the Earth is still in motion, and she will never pass away on Earth. She will always remain on Earth until the time comes when the Earth will end. She will suffer on Earth. Now when the Earth will come to an end, she will burn with it." So this is what the messengers said.

And so Handsome Lake said, "Now this woman's Indian name is 'Big Woman' (Agúwanen Agóngweh)."

Missionaries
(Dahénneh Hadijihén:stajih)

This part is about the coming of the early missionaries:

The messengers said to Handsome Lake, "Now look and watch."

They pointed toward the east where the sun rises. So he did look that way. Something black was coming slowly. It looked like a man coming. The object in black was coming closer this way.

The messengers asked, "What did you see and observe?"

He replied, "There is something black coming this way. It looks like a man in black clothes who is coming."

Then they replied, "It is true, you are right in the way you observed and understood. There are missionaries coming and bringing Christianity and education.

"So we think when they arrive they will try to persuade your people to accept their religion and that is going to cause many different opinions among your people.

"So this will happen when they arrive. So now the chiefs should encourage your relations and warn them to be cautious about this important matter and not to accept it."

Strong Drink
(*Ohné:gah*)

This part is about the continual making of strong drinks:

The messengers said, "Take a close look in that direction toward the east where the sun rises."

So he did look in that direction. Then they said to him, "What did you see? What did you observe?"

He replied, "It seems that there is smoke rising as far as I can see. It seems there are buildings of some kind and people are working there."

So the messengers said to him, "It is true, you are right what you saw. You have seen the place where they make the strong drink.

"We hear the people saying, 'I will not quit until I drink up all the strong drinks.'

"So we think and feel that what your people are saying will never happen and cannot be done. The strong drink is too great and they are continually making more strong drink and there will be no end of it."

Red Jacket
(*Shagoyehwá:thá*)

This part is about Shagoyehwá:thá, the one the white man called Red Jacket.

The messengers said to Handsome Lake, "Watch closely in the direction of the northeast."

So he did look in that direction. He saw a man. It seemed as if he was moving earth, that he faced many hardships and was suffering. Steam seemed to be coming out of his body. It also seemed that he was perspiring.

So the messengers said, "What did you see?"

Then he replied, "It seems that the man is moving earth. He is perspiring, and it looks as if steam is coming out of his body."

So the messengers replied, "That one you saw is a man who has given his consent to sell Indian land. That is an old Indian trail that leads to Split Basswood Tree, an old Indian settlement. It is now known as Buffalo, New York. This man's name was 'He-who-wakes-up-everyone,' or Red Jacket.*

"So the one you saw is a man. He is punished because he has done a great wrong to the Creator. That is the way he will suffer as long as the Earth is in motion."

This is the way the messengers were showing things to our great leader. So this is the way he used to tell it.

The Red Jacket
(*Shagoyehwá:thá*)

This part is about an angry man wearing a red coat:

The messengers said, "Look and watch closely in that direction, about the middle of the sky."

---

* Handsome Lake was told by the Celestial Beings that Red Jacket had done a great wrong in selling land which was not his. The land belongs to the Creator and the coming faces, unborn.

It is said that if you sell your land, it is like selling your mother's body. Our ancestors always respected their mothers and they respected Mother Earth.

The followers of the Good Message to this day mention the name of Red Jacket with contempt. While they acknowledge his wisdom, they have no other admiration for him. He was a fiery warrior who had announced that the Creator had made known to him in a dream that the Seneca Nation would never prosper until they made him a chief. He was the enemy of Cornplanter and had frequent collisions with Handsome Lake and recognized him only as an imposter.

So again he did look. He saw a white man pacing back and forth. He seemed to be angry about something. He was prodding the ground with a bayonet and wearing a red jacket or coat.

The messengers said to him, "What did you see?"

He replied, "I saw a man and it seems he is angry about something. He is holding a bayonet or fork, and he is prodding the ground with it."

Then the messengers said, "It is true what you saw. We think and feel that there will be many people who will die if he does not settle down. We are hoping he will change his mind. He is thinking of war. If war does start, tell your relations not to get involved in this conflict. We understand that there are two white brothers arguing, and the only way this will be settled is by war."

The messengers continued, "Do not let your relations take sides. If they do, they will suffer and lose their homelands. So tell your chiefs not to let this happen to your people." This is how the messengers and Handsome Lake told it.

He Who Refused to Relate the Creator's Words (*Ahaihwahtsha:don*)

The Creator had given a certain man a duty. He was to relate a message to the people on Earth about how they should live from now on.

The messengers said to Handsome Lake, "Look and watch closely in that direction around the middle, between the west and the south."

So again he did look that way. It seemed there was a valley between two hills, and at the foot of the hill there was a heap of dirt. It looked as if a man was buried there. It seemed as if it was very hot and there was steam coming out of the ground where a body was buried.

So the messengers said to him, "What did you see?"

Handsome Lake said, "It seems there is a valley between the two hills and at the foot of the hill a man is buried. It is very hot there and steam is coming out of that heap of dirt."

Then the messengers said, "It is true the way you saw it. It was a man who was buried there. He did not relate the Good Message to your relations. He was given a duty to tell the Good Message to the people. But he did not fulfill his duty and he disobeyed the Creator."

So this is the way they showed him things when they were relating the evil things on Earth to him.

The Animals Become Extinct (*Godí:nyo:Gennathahí:neh*)

This part is about the animals being restless as they walk along:

The messengers said to him, "Look and watch closely toward the southeast."

So again he looked and watched closely. He saw the deer and the bear walking, and they seemed restless.

So the messengers said to him, "What did you see and observe?"

He replied, "I saw the animals walking along, and they seemed restless."

The messengers said to him, "It is true what you saw. The people on Earth have too much sin, that is why the animals are so restless. These animals have no place to go for protection. The water is polluted and the Earth is too hot because there is so much sin on Earth. These animals will also become extinct."

Those Who Disobey the Good Message (*Ondadenhodón:kwa*)

This part is about a place where people go if they disobey the rules of the white man:

The messengers said, "Look and watch closely."

They pointed back down to Earth. So again he looked back down on Earth. There was a huge building standing there, and it seemed that it was strong and sturdy. Inside the building there were things like hand-cuffs, a whip, and a rope. The rope was used to hang people.

So the messengers said to him, "What did you see?"

Handsome Lake replied, "I saw a large building. It was a sturdy house and in it lay a whip, hand-cuffs, and a rope."

Then the messengers said to him, "It is where the white man punishes a person who does wrong, and it is called a jail house.

"We think your people will also be punished there. Whoever does wrong things and disobeys the white man and also those who do not honour the Good Message will suffer there."

The White Man's Way
(*Ondrennaén:dakwa*)

This part is about a church:

The messengers said, "Look and watch closely at a certain place down on Earth."

So he did look back down on Earth. There was a house standing there, where the white race meet and pray. It looked as if the house was white, with a spire on the roof. It had no door and no windows, and no road led out of the house.

Inside the house was a great noise of people praying. They were calling the Creator by name. Handsome Lake heard the voices of his own relations praying.

So the messengers said to him, "What did you observe?"

He said, "I saw a white house with a spire on it. There were people in it, and it looked like a meeting place for the white race. The house has no door and no windows, and there is no road leading anywhere. I heard loud voices of people praying. I also heard the voices of my relations coming from that house."

So again the messengers said to him, "You are right. It is true what you saw. So that is the place where the white race meet and pray.

"So this is what will happen. We think and feel that many of your people will follow the ways of the white race. They will be convinced to take the white man's belief and go to church.

"So when the Earth burns, those who embrace the beliefs of the Bible will suffer with the white race. Also it is going to be a hard matter for your people who are persuaded and convinced to embrace Christianity to come back to the Good Message. This kind of belief does not belong to the native people. It was meant only for the white race."

The Longhouse
(Ganónh:se:s)

This part is about the Longhouse:

The messengers said, "Now look and watch closely."

So again he did look back down on Earth. There stood a house which looked like a longhouse. A road led out of the doorway of the house and ascended to the sky.

Again the messengers said to him, "What did you see?"

Handsome Lake said, "I see a house. It is a longhouse, and there is a road going out from the doorway, which ascends to the sky."

Then the messengers said to him. "It is true the way you observed what you saw. The house you saw is a longhouse. There is a road descending from the sky, which leads to the doorway. There is a reason for this. If anyone is able to fulfill the Good Message and has repented of all their sins and has been forgiven by the Creator, they will follow the path that leads to the land of the Creator.

The Alcoholic
(*Ohné:gah*)

*This part is about a man who likes to drink
strong drink — ohné:gah.*

The messengers said to Handsome Lake, "Look below on Earth."

So again he looked down on Earth. A house was standing there, and two men came out of the house. One man was escorting the other man.

They walked for a way on the road, then turned back again and went back inside the house. The one man was staggering as he walked back into the house. This kept happening. They would go so far and turn back and go into the house again.

So the messengers said to him, "Now what did you see?"

Then he replied, "There is a house standing there. Two men came out of the house. One was assisted by the other man and they were walking arm in arm. The one man was staggering and his body was wobbling. They would only go so far and then turn back. They would go back into the house again."

So the messengers said to our leader, "It is true the way you saw it. So the one you saw is the man who uses strong drink. Now you see what strong drink has done to him. He cannot control his mind anymore.

"When he thinks of leaving to go home he only goes so far and turns back. He goes back to the same place. So that house you saw is the place where they sell strong drinks (a hotel).

"These two men have been friends for a long time. They have agreed that they will always be together no matter what happens. But one day one of the men became ill and died. The one left was now only able to go to his friend's grave. What they had said to one another was not true. The friend left behind could not go with his friend beneath the earth. These men were only drinking friends and this is not the right way for friends to be."

The Roads

This part is about the forked path (deyohthahó:gen).

The messengers said, "We will now continue on our journey. We will go to the place where the path divides.* This is the place where the human race will go when they leave Mother Earth."

---

* The great sky-road of the *Gaiwí:yo:* (the Good Message) is the Milky Way. The souls of the dead are supposed to journey along this sky-road, which heads towards a fork. The multitude of stars are thought to be the number of souls of the dead. The narrow road leads to the land of the Creator. This is where people go after death if they have repented of all the wrong things in their life according to the teachings of *Gaiwí:yo:*, the Good Message of the Creator.

This is the way Handsome Lake used to say it:

So we arrived at the place where the path divides.

One path was wide, leading out, and there were mostly adult footprints on it. This wider path led to the place of punishment.

The other path was narrow. There were more children's footprints on this path.

When we arrived at the forked path, there were two men standing there. One was the Evil Spirit's helper. The other, who stood on the other side of the narrow path, was the Creator's helper.

During the time we stood there the two men were arguing about which way a woman would go when she arrived. It was not long before someone came along the pathway. It was a woman, and she was running as she came near the forked path. The Evil Spirit's helper began to talk.

He said, "This is the way she will go because she has fulfilled all the wicked and evil things on Earth." So when she arrived and stood there, the Evil Spirit's helper said to her, "This is the way you will go." It seemed that she could not control herself because she was pulled by a force that made her go that way.

In a few moments someone else came along the path. It was another woman. When she arrived, she stood there, and the Creator's helper said, "This is the way she will go because she has repented of all her sins on Earth."

Again the Evil Spirit's helper said, "It is not right. It is too soon. It was only a few days ago that she repented."

The Creator's helper said, "It is true that she repented only a few days ago, but she has fulfilled the Good Message. She said, 'I repent of all my sins and will keep it that way as long as I live here on Earth.' So she will go this way."

This is what our great leader used to say: The messengers had to stand in front of her and escort her onto the narrow path. Then she was able to go toward the land of the Creator.

The Narrow Path
(*Niyohahoó:ooh*)

Handsome Lake looked toward the narrow path that leads to the land of the Creator. It seemed it was not very often that an adult passed by and went that way. Those who passed by were mostly little children. The place where the path divided seemed very narrow.

So the messengers said to him, "You looked that way toward the wide path. What did you see?"

He replied, "I am surprised that the path is so wide and that there are so many adults and so few children who have gone that way.

The messengers said to him, "This is the place where the people are separated when they arrive here. That place (the Milky Way) is where many people will pass by when they leave Earth."

The Human Soul

*The following ideas about the human soul are the ancient truths
held by the Iroquois. Their influence on the teachings of
Handsome Lake will be noted upon reading the Gaiwí:yo:.*

Every soul retains its personal identity, whatever form it may inhabit.

Soul differs from spirit.

When the soul leaves the body, the spirit generally does as well. However, it does not necessarily leave it and if it does, it may not leave immediately. It may linger for one year.

When the spirit passes from a living body, it may enter any object or go to any place to acquire wisdom and, returning, reveal this wisdom to the person from whose body it came, in dreams or visions.

Should a person persistently refuse to heed these warning visions, the spirit is liable to desert him, leaving him simply a creature without power to resist or understand the influence of the various directions of good or bad.

People who think that they may lose their spirits because of some oversight or evildoing often offer sacrifices to the Evil Spirit. By offering a sacrifice, the person will survive because he or she will have satisfied the Evil Spirit.

The House of Punishment
(*Ganóngeh Shagohewátha' Thononh:soht*)

This part is about the House of Punishment.

The messengers said to our great leader, "Now we will continue on our journey. We will go to the House of Punishment. We will also have to walk along the pathway. This would be better for us."

So this is the way Handsome Lake used to say it:

As things appeared, there was a slope on a hill. We had

almost reached the top of the hill when we began to feel a draft of hot air coming from the direction we were headed.

Then we reached the top of the hill and I began to notice there was another slope going down. So we began to go down the hill. At the bottom of the hill there was a house. The house looked as if it had been red hot some time ago and had since cooled off.

Then the messengers said to me, "Now you have seen the place where a person will be punished by the punisher if he does not fulfill the Good Message.

"What you saw is true. We thought we would bring you here to see for yourself what it is like at the House of Punishment. We thought we would show you the truth of what we are relating to you for you to tell your relations on Earth."

Handsome Lake used to say:

This is the way I saw the House of Punishment: the roof of the house looked very hot; it looked like hot vapour rising from the Earth's surface in the summertime.

Now one of the messengers pulled something out of his pocket. It looked like glass or quartz. He pointed the object toward the house and he raised the house to the height of a person or maybe a little higher. The house was filled with people.

The people noticed that we were looking at them, and this is what happened. They all looked our way. Their unhappy faces showed that they were suffering. They wanted me to help them out of that place.

Then the messengers said to me, "What did you observe? What did you see?"

I replied, "The way I saw it, the people wanted me to help them get out of the place."

So now the messengers said, "It is true what happened. But you cannot help them. It is too late for them now. When they were still on Earth that was the time and place for you to have helped them."

Our great leader used to say:

I saw a man walking the length of the house. It seemed that he was the master of the house. His movements changed so quickly. His whole appearance changed. Sometimes he had features like a horse, sometimes he had feet like a horse's feet and then sometimes his feet were like a cow's feet. He also had horns on his head.

The messengers spoke: "It is true what you have seen. He is the master of the house. That is the Punisher you saw walking around. He is the one you call the Evil Spirit. He is the one who will punish the people who refuse to fulfill the Good Message. Look and watch closely."

Handsome Lake watched and heard the master of the house calling a man's name. He seemed to know his name. So he called him by the name he used while he was still on Earth.

He said, "Come here, my nephew."

In a few moments the man came out of the crowd of people in the house and stood before him. He said to him, "Now it is time for you to drink again."

There was a kettle with something boiling in it. It looked like lead or melted iron and it was red hot. He gave him a cup of drink.

He said to him, "Now you will drink this."

The man did not want to drink it, but it seemed that he had no control. It was as if something forced him to drink it anyway. Smoke came out of his mouth and from all over his body. He screamed out with great pain. He said, "I repent."

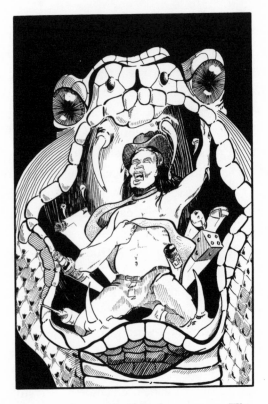

Then the punisher said, "Just keep it up. This was your delight. You always liked to drink while you were still on Earth and you were always hollering. So come on, holler again. That is what you liked to do when you were drinking."

Then he called another person. He called her by her name. He said, "Come here, my niece." He used her given name, the name she used while she was still living on Earth.

It was not long before she came out of the crowd and stood in front of him. Then he grabbed her and put her into the kettle. He pushed her down inside the kettle and she came back up again screaming. It sounded like an animal or creature screaming.

Again he pushed her back down into the kettle. When she emerged from the bottom of the kettle, she said, "Would you please let me cool off? It is very hot in here."

So then he grabbed her and jerked her out of the kettle and put her into the other kettle. It looked as if it contained ice cold water.

In a short time, when she emerged, she said, "Would you please let me out? I want to warm up."

So the Evil Spirit said, "You are never satisfied."

So again he pulled her out of the kettle and dunked her into the other kettle, where it was boiling.

The messengers said to Handsome Lake, "What did it look like? What did you observe?"

He told the messengers the things he had seen.

Then the messengers said, "It is true what you saw. That is the kind of punishment received by those who practise witchcraft and who do not repent before they leave the Earth."

Then the Evil Spirit said again, "Both of you, come here, my nephew and my niece."

He called out the names of two people — a man and his wife. They came out of the crowd and stood before him.

The Evil Spirit said, "You are to start an argument. This is what you liked to do all the time that you were both still living on Earth."

So they began to argue, even though they did not want to argue. While they were arguing, sparks and fire came out of their mouths. They argued and argued until they were unable to argue anymore. Their eyeballs began to bulge out and their tongues began to hang out. They were both screaming and suffering.

The messengers said to our leader, "What did you see?"

He told the messengers the things he had seen.

They said to him, "It is true what you saw, how the people are punished, a husband and wife who like to argue a lot."

So this is the way Handsome Lake saw it while he was on a journey with the Celestial Beings. This is how he told it to his people.

Again the Evil Spirit said, "Nephew, come here." He knew this person's name so well. He called him by the name he used while he was still on Earth.

It was not long before the man came out of the crowd and stood before him. Again the Punisher said to the man. "You will have fun and a good time. This was your delight while you were still on Earth. It was your custom to beat up your wife. You will start to beat her up."

There stood a statue of a woman. The statue looked as if it was made of iron. He went toward it and began to beat it up. It seemed he could not refuse, that he was forced by the Punisher to beat up the statue.

He could not control himself. He was screaming. He kept saying, "I repent now." He kept repeating it until his voice began to fade away.

The Punisher said to him, "Keep it up. This is what gave you pleasure when you beat up your wife and abused people."

So this is the way things were when the messengers were showing Handsome Lake around.

The messengers ended by saying, "You have seen the kind of punishment that any man will receive if he abuses his wife as well as other human beings. The Creator never meant human beings to abuse one another."

The Punisher said to another man, "Come here, nephew."

The man came out of the crowd immediately and stood before him.

The Punisher continued, "Now you will have a good time. This was your custom and delight. You played the violin and you also liked to drink. So now you will have a wonderful time."

The Punisher handed him something that looked like a short, red-hot iron. He said, "Now play the violin and sing." The cords on his arms were the strings of the instrument that would make the music.

He began to play by rubbing the hot iron on his arm. The tendons on his arm made the music. It seemed that he could not control himself. He was in agony and screaming. He was giving up.

He kept saying, "I repent of all my sins." He kept repeating this until his voice began to fade away. The Punisher kept encouraging him not to give up, shouting, "Stay with it. Do not give up. It was your custom and delight during the time you were still on Earth."

So that is how things were when Handsome Lake was on a journey with the messengers showing him the House of Punishment.

This part is about the people who have the custom of playing card games.

Again the Evil Spirit said, "Come here, my nephews." This time two men immediately came out of the crowd and stood before him as he called out their names.

Then the Punisher said, "Now you will both play cards.

That was your custom and delight on Earth." He gave them a set of cards which seemed to be made of metal.

Then they began to play. It seemed as if the cards were red hot. Sparks began to fly while they were playing.

The Punisher said, "Stay with it, it was your custom and delight while you were still living on Earth."

The messengers said to Handsome Lake, "What did you see?"

He told them what he had seen and observed. Then the messengers said, "It is true what you observed. So what you saw is the kind of punishment your people will suffer when they play card games and fail to repent of their sins on Earth."

Discipline
(*Thenh Deondadahí:stán:nih Né Ondathá:wahk*)

*This part is about a mother who did not discipline and punish her children the right way.**

So again our great leader looked toward the House of Punishment. He saw a large kettle sitting on hot coals and

---

* Handsome Lake respected and cared for children. There are many instances in the *Gaiwí:yo:* relating to the care and rearing of children. The mode of punishment referred to here was one of long usage. Sometimes the mother would take a container and fill it up with cold water and splash it onto the child. This would be repeated until obedience was enforced. The mother who was entrusted with the care of children was accustomed to telling her children what was wrong and allowing them by experience to know that her word was to be relied upon.

A boy remained under the discipline of his mother until the age of puberty, when he was turned over to his grandfather for training. If the boy was unruly or without ambition the mother and father would ask the elders to talk to their son. The boy would also be disciplined by his father's parents.

there was some kind of liquid boiling in it. Suddenly there appeared two people, a mother and daughter, from the bottom of the kettle.

·Now the child said to her mother, "This is a hard matter."

The mother said to the daughter, "It is true what I was trying to tell you. I scolded you for your wrongdoings, but you never listened to me."

The child said to the mother, "You should have scolded me more and punished me with a red whip."

Then they were forced down to the bottom of the kettle again by the Punisher.

The messengers said, "What you saw is the way they will be punished if the mother does not demand what she tells her children for their own good."

So this is the way things were when the messengers were taking him on a journey to see things for himself.

Abortion
(*Godadwiyáh: dondonh*)

This part is about a woman who has taken something so she will not bear any children.

The Punisher said, "Come here, my niece." So the woman came out of the crowd and stood before him.

Right away she noticed there was someone else close by, watching. The expression on her face showed she was embarrassed about her appearance because she was naked.

There appeared to be all kinds of roots and herbs attached to her. It was actually more like a string of children which she was dragging along the ground. It was coming out from between her legs. It seemed that these were the many children she would have borne.

So again the messengers said to our great leader, "This is how a person will be punished if she administers medicine to cut off birth and prevents herself from bearing children."

This part is about native people who take delight in white people's dances.

Now the Punisher said, "I command you to come here, my nephews." So soon, several men came out of the crowd and stood before him.

So the Punisher said to the men, "Now you will enjoy yourselves. You always enjoyed dancing while you were on Earth. It was your delight. You liked dancing the white man's dances, known as square dancing. So you will dance."

So they did dance.

This is what our great leader used to say:

It seemed that the floor was all metal. As they danced, there were sparks flying and they were suffering. They were crying and they were not able to do anything about it.

The Punisher said, "Stay with it. It is fun. I have always been saying it is fun in my house."

The messengers said to Handsome Lake, "Now you saw the kind of punishment your relations will receive if they like dancing the white man's dances."

A woman was thinking about having new experiences. She desired to know men.

The Punisher said, "Come here, my niece." He called her

by the name she was called while she was still living on Earth. It was not long before she came out of the crowd and stood before him.

He said to her, "This was your custom and delight to have new experiences with men. You always desired to know more men. So now your desire will be fulfilled. It was your delight while you were still on Earth."

So now he forced a hot iron rod in the shape of a man's penis on her and she was not able to do anything about it. It seemed as if she was suffering from great pain.

She was screaming for help and said, "I repent."

The Punisher said to her, "Keep it up, this was your delight."

He grabbed another hot iron rod. Now this one was even more painful. She suffered more as he forced it on her. So he continued to force this on her until her voice began to die out. Then she fell to the floor. It seemed as if smoke came out from all over her body.

So this is the way things were when the messengers showed our leader the House of Punishment.

This part is about a man who says he will kill the Evil Spirit when he arrives at the Evil Spirit's house.

So the Punisher said, "Come here, my nephew." In a few minutes a man came out of the crowd and stood before him.

The Punisher said, "Now you have arrived here. While you were still on Earth, you said, 'I am going to kill the Evil Spirit when I arrive at his house.' So now you have arrived here. Now you can kill me."

The man could not do anything. He was unable to do what he had always said he would do. The Punisher challenged him.

He said, "Stay with it. You always said you would kill me when you arrived at my house. So now it is true you have arrived here. So kill me and do it now."

The man was unable to do anything. He was unable to do the things he used to say he would do while he was still on Earth.

So the messengers said to Handsome Lake:

Now you have seen the House of Punishment where the people go, those who never repented when they were still on Earth.

"So this is the truth, the evil things you have seen on Earth. The one you saw is the Punisher. It will be up to him how long he plays with, punishes, and tortures a person. He has the power to bring a person back to life again after the person has already been turned to ashes.

"He will gather the ashes of a person and return him to life again. He will start over and torture the person again after he has already turned him to ashes once. It will be up to the Punisher to decide when he will give up — he may turn the person to ashes again. Then he will blow the ashes away and dispose of them forever."

So now the messengers said to our leader, "We have shown you all the evil things people can do and the kind of punishment they will get if they fail to repent when they pass away on Earth. That will be enough for now."

The Land of the Creator
(*Thaonhwenjá:deh Shongwaiatíhs:on*)

The messengers said, "We will continue on our journey. We will go to the land of the Creator."

They continued on their journey. Suddenly Handsome Lake noticed something coming toward them. Our leader understood what it was. As they walked along, it became clearer that a dog was coming. The dog was running. It began to wag its tail, it was so happy to see him.

Then the messengers said to him, "That is the dog you considered for the Midwinter Ceremony, which the Creator has given you and sanctioned Himself. So that is your dog."

They took up their journey again. As they moved along, it got brighter. A more brilliant light appeared. Our leader could smell a beautiful fragrance of flowers and a fragrance of many different varieties of fruit.

Many different kinds of birds were flying around him that he had never seen before. They were so beautiful.

So now they entered the land of the Creator. Along the pathway he saw some berries growing. Wild strawberries.

Then the messengers said to him, "You will not eat the berries now. There will eventually come a time when you will eat them. Someday you will eat the berries when you arrive here."

So they proceeded on their journey. They arrived at a place where small trees and bushes had overgrown the land. There on the other side of these small trees and bushes was a clearing like a grassy place.

He heard the voice of a man. He understood who it was.

It seemed as if he was announcing that a lacrosse game (*gajihgwá:e:*) would be played early the next morning. Our leader recognized the man's voice.

Then the messengers said to our leader, "The voice you heard is Johahí:seh. That was his custom when he was still on Earth. All his life he was faithful to his beliefs and respected the Good Message. That is the reason he will continue his duty when he arrives in the land of the Creator. He repented of all his sins on Earth before he passed away."

So our leader heard the announcement that a lacrosse game would be played here tomorrow around noontime and that Awenhén:seh ("New Flower") would be the one to face off the game.

Our leader knew that Awenhén:seh was still living on Earth. Would he arrive here by noontime tomorrow to face it off? Our leader thought he would see what would happen tomorrow at noontime.

And it came true. At noontime Awenhén:seh passed away on Earth as predicted.

Now the messengers said to Handsome Lake, "We have now come to this point. So now we will leave it up to you if you wish to go and visit your mother in that house over there. We will stand here and wait for you until you return."

So he went to visit his mother.

When he arrived at the house, he went in. But his mother was not home. Only his niece was home.

She said, "You have arrived, my uncle."

Handsome Lake replied, "Not yet, I have just come to visit for a short time."

Then she said, "Do you see that thing hanging over there? You gave it to me when I left the Earth below."

He saw it hanging there and recognized it. It was a bleached fawn skin that he had used to wrap the cornbread that she was to take on her journey to the spirit world.

Now his niece said to him, "Your mother is not home. She has gone over to that house."

He went back where the messengers stood. They proceeded on their journey, but had not gone far when suddenly they noticed a man coming toward them. He stood on the opposite side of the pathway. Then they stopped.

Now the man said, "Did you ever hear any of your ancestors say that once upon a time there was a man visiting on Earth and it was the Great Spirit's son?"

Handsome Lake said, "Yes, I used to hear them sometimes talk about him. Is it true what they used to say?"

He said, "It is true. I was there. I was sent by my Father to deliver the Good Message to the blue-eyed people over the Great Saltwater. They think that they have killed me, but it is not true. They never killed me. I only came home."

"So it came true. We have now met. I often hear your relations saying that you talk to ghosts."

"What they said came true. So now it is true what the people on Earth are talking about. They thought they'd killed me. Here, look at me, here are the marks where the spikes were driven into my hands and feet when they hung me on a cross. Now that was the time I left and came home.

"How about you, did the people accept your teachings?"

Handsome Lake replied, "It seems that half the people honour and accept the Good Message."

So now the Fourth Messenger said, "You have done better than I. You are successful. Your people have grasped the Good Message, but with me, not one person would believe or accept the good things I talked about. The people of the white race think they have killed me. It is not true, I just came home. So when I arrived home in the land of the Creator, I left everything to my Father.

"I said to my Father, 'Now it will be up to You to decide what You will do about it. You saw what the white race did to me.'

"Then my Father said, 'I leave everything to you. You went through this yourself and suffered.'

"Then I said, 'Not a single soul of the white race will rise and go to the land of the Creator.'"

The Fourth Messenger said to Handsome Lake, "Half the people seem to believe and honour the Good Message. I think it will happen to you some day. Your relations will refuse to listen to your teachings. You will be neglected and they will not honour the Good Message."

The Great Web
(*Odahá:deh Deyohtahadé:nyon*)

This part is about an object like webbing revolving in the sky.

The messengers said, "Now you will see a webbing revolving slowly."

So now they proceeded on their journey. They arrived where there was a huge object like a web revolving slowly. It seemed that it was where the circulating air begins.

The messengers said to Handsome Lake, "You saw the place where the circulation of air on Earth originated. We are always watching it closely so that it always stays at the same speed as it turns. We think that if it turns too fast many of your relations will be destroyed by it. It would take a wide sweep across the Earth and it would be disastrous and cause much destruction to the Earth."

So that is the way things were when they showed it to our great leader.

The Balance of Mother Earth

This part is about two round objects that look like raindrops hanging in mid-air. One drop is yellow and one is red.

The messengers said, "Look over there."

They pointed it out. So Handsome Lake looked and saw

two drops which seemed to be hanging in the sky, and they were going to drop any time. Both drops were round, but each had a different colour. One was red and the other was yellow. So that is the way our leader saw it.

Now the messengers said, "It would not be a good thing if it were to happen some day that the two drops hanging there dropped and landed on Earth. We think and feel it would bring a great calamity among your people. It would destroy many people. So that is the reason we are trying our best to keep it under control at all times.

"If it does happen — it is now known when it may happen — you should prepare for this. It is a terminal disease. If either one of these round drops falls and lands on Earth, it will cause great calamity to your people. So that is the reason your people should be prepared.

"We recommend that every person should have some snapping turtle's liver and loon's liver. It should be dried and made into powder. This will be available for use at any time. No time can be wasted to look for that kind of medicine whenever this will happen."

This is what the messengers showed him during their journey in the sky-world.

The Last Days of the Journey
(*Shonwahtgáh:wen Onhwénjageh Ne Sganyadaí:yoh*)

So they took up their journey again and after a time the Four Messengers said, "We have arrived at the point where you must return. Over there is a house prepared for your eternal abode, but should you now enter the room, you could never go back to the Earth world."

Handsome Lake chose to continue his journey so he could preach the Good Message to his people.

Now when Handsome Lake arrived at Tonawanda, having come from Burnt House (Dyononhsadé:genh), he was determined to complete his mission.

He had started his journey by preaching for ten years at Cornplanter's village, then he preached for two years at Cold Spring and four years at Tonawanda. While at Tonawanda, he received an invitation from the Onondaga asking him to come and preach the Good Message to the people, chiefs, and leaders of their nation.

Now it happened that the Four Messengers appeared to him when the invitation was extended and they related their message to Handsome Lake. The messengers said, "They are your own people at Onondaga. Let this be the way. Prepare yourself and cleanse your body with medicine. It is necessary, moreover, for you to find yourself in some secret spot in the forest and await our call to start.

"You will meet a chief by the name of Hawenaseh ("New Voice"). You will be bidden the third time to sing his song and this will be the last."

Handsome Lake replied, "There is nothing now to stop me from fulfilling my call. I must now take up my final journey to the new world." He thought for a while and was greatly troubled and longed for the home of his childhood.

Handsome Lake and New Voice met, and the chief urged the prophet to accept the invitation of his friends and relatives. He said, "The people are waiting with open arms to see you coming. I will go forth to the gathering of chiefs at Buffalo Creek and tell them you are on your way."

So Handsome Lake started on his journey. A large number of people followed him on foot. They, too, wanted to hear him speak.

In time they came to a camping place called Ganawágaes (meaning "A Swamp with a Strong Odour"), and Handsome Lake said to his followers in a commanding voice, "Assemble early in the morning."

The next day he spoke to them and shared a dream. In his dream he had seen a pathway, a trail overgrown and covered with grass so that it appeared not to have been travelled on in a long time.

They continued on their journey. The next campsite was near Ganadahsé:geh (meaning "New Village," or "New Town"). There he gathered the people together again and gave thanks and shared another dream with his followers.

He said, "I heard in a dream a certain woman speaking, but I am not able to say whether she was from Onondaga or Tonawanda from where we came."

They proceeded on their journey. When they had reached the outskirts of Tonawanda, he said to his followers, "Let us refresh ourselves before going any farther." So they rested and ate before continuing on their journey. In a little while, Handsome Lake realized he had forgotten his knife. He turned to his followers and said, "I cannot lose that knife because I prize it very much. I must return to our last stopping place and find it."

He told his followers to continue on to the village, and he returned to the last stopping place alone. Handsome Lake found his knife, but unknown to him a curse had been placed on the knife by a witch. Upon his return to the village, he took ill and was in great distress. His colleagues saw that he was approaching slowly and escorted him into the Longhouse.

Seeing his state of health, the people offered to play a game of lacrosse to cheer him up. It was a bright and beautiful day and they took Handsome Lake back outside to watch the game, but soon he asked to be taken back inside the Longhouse.

Once inside, he began to speak to his followers. "I will soon go to my new home. I will step into the spirit world, for there is a path before me leading there. So whoever follows my teachings will follow in my footsteps and I will look back upon them with outstretched arms, inviting them into the land of the Creator. It will become foggy on the path when I am gone and I hope that someone will follow my tracks and fulfill the Good Message. But I hope that when I am gone, all may uphold and believe in the Good Message." So this is what our great leader Sganyadaí:yoh said to his people.

Chief Jacob Thomas tells the story this way: "The prophet taught the message for nearly sixteen years. During that time he taught at Burnt House, Cold Springs, and Tonawanda. It was at Tonawanda that he received the invitation to go to Onondaga, New York. On the day he left, many followers went with him. They were soon camped near the village of Onondaga. During the night Handsome Lake heard the voice of a woman who spoke to him saying, "You are coming to the village to criticize us for practising witchcraft." Handsome Lake could not tell from what direction the voice was coming. This is all he heard.

"The next morning they headed out for the village. Later in the day Handsome Lake realized he had left his knife behind at the campsite. A knife to a man was a very worthwhile thing, so Handsome Lake left his followers and returned for the knife. When he rejoined his followers he was quite ill. His followers thought a curse had been placed on him through his knife. Handsome Lake passed away that day in the Longhouse of the Onondaga village.

"Some people suspected he had been cursed because he had been speaking out against alcohol, witchcraft, love potions, and abortion. Many people did not like his teachings and went against the message. They could not face the truth. The people were angry and the witches did their work. Handsome Lake was dead.

"Many of the old people often said that at that time there were powerful witches who did not approve of Handsome Lake and his teachings. His message interfered with their evil practices. The Celestial Messengers had warned him to be careful of this prediction.

Handsome Lake died on August 10, 1815, at Onondaga. The Code was not preached for nine years after his death. Many people turned back to alcohol, and many families began to suffer from violence because of the drinking. The Seneca women, seeing this, began to revive the preachings of Handsome Lake, and every year since then it has been preached at the Six Nations near Brantford, Ontario, and in New York State.

It is possible that in the near future the Code may be lost, in the sense that it will not be heard in its original tongue, since most of the young people no longer speak their native language.

The Teachings of
Chief Jacob Thomas

CHIEF JACOB THOMAS LEANED back in his chair and
seemed to be remembering something from the past.
He paused for a few moments to collect those thoughts. He
is definitely a man of the oral tradition. Everything is recalled
by way of story. He himself is a story, a story revealing old
ways. It seems to me there are few men remaining on the
Earth Mother like Chief Thomas. Who will be able to walk
in his moccasins? I wondered. Chief Thomas continued.

After the death of Handsome Lake, many of the
Hotinónshon:ni returned to the old ways of practising
witchcraft and abortion, using love potions, and drinking
alcohol. After nine years, a group of Seneca women
gathered to discuss the need to return to the Code of
Handsome Lake. The women approached the elders and
chiefs to find someone who could remember the Code.
One man was found who had followed Handsome Lake,
and with co-operative efforts the Code was resurrected.
A great fire was burned to let the smoke rise, to show the

people of the Six Nations that the Code of Handsome Lake was still alive.

From that time a fire has burned and the women of the clan nations (clan mothers) have upheld the Code of Handsome Lake. Each year the Code of Handsome Lake is recited to the people. As the Code is followed, it will help the Hotinónshon:ni rebuild lives that have been devastated by wrong living. One of the worst destroyers, said Chief Thomas, has been alcohol.

"The Europeans did not know the damage alcohol would do to native people," he said. Alcohol was something that the elders knew about after they had studied it for some time. The Europeans brought alcohol, diseases, Christianity, and education. Alcohol continues to cause violence and abuse, the neglect of children, and the beating of women and men in native society.

Chief Thomas remained subdued for some time after speaking about alcohol. He is greatly saddened by the effect alcohol has on his people. He sees it every day on the reserve near Brantford, Ontario, where he lives. Jake is clear on the subject of alcohol as it is stated in the Code of Handsome Lake. Alcohol was not given to native people but to the white man by the Creator. It was to be used as medicine, but the white man has also come to abuse it.

"When I was a child," he recalled, "I would hear about the effects of alcohol on a native person. My grandmother would tell my sister that one day she would marry and have children. She would tell her that if she drank, it would not be good because the alcohol would go to her bloodstream and eventually to the child she would carry. There is no cure once the alcohol has been transmitted to the baby, to its blood, and to its bone marrow. This will be carried for seven generations. Today we call this fetal alcohol syndrome. But even back then the elders knew of this. Did the Europeans have to bring alcohol to our people? It has spoiled our lives for generation after generation and still it continues today."

The French, English, and Dutch fur traders were responsible for the breakup of the nations. The French were mainly responsible for introducing Christianity. The British and the French sought allegiance from the natives, and this helped to create many wars among the native peoples. The Hurons, the Iroquois, and the Algonquins fought amongst themselves for control of the fur trade. According to Jake, contrary to common belief, it was the whites who introduced scalping at this time.

From the time of the fur trade, there was a bitter feud among nations. The Hurons were Iroquois and one of the first nations to organize the Confederacy, but the introduction of the fur trade resulted in the Hurons breaking up their own Confederacy.

In those days the native people ventured to the white settlements to trade their pelts for alcohol. When the hunters came back upstream to return to their villages in present-day New York State, they would be drinking and yelling. Their people could hear them from a great distance. The women knew the hunters were under the influence of alcohol and would take the children and hide away from the villages; they would build shelters for their families and would listen for days and nights to the dogs barking and the men yelling while they drank alcohol. Many hunters died as a result of fighting amongst themselves. Their homes would be ransacked, the doors knocked out, and the fires allowed to die

out. The women returned after all the alcohol was consumed only to be greeted by dead bodies laid out for burial. After this the native people would try to resume a normal life again until the next trading season.

This was the origin of violence among the people and of abuse within families. Those who did not drink alcohol suffered anyway because they saw their way of life changing as a result of the Europeans' influence. It was predicted at that time that this would happen. The native people never did change back to the old ways. Alcoholism remains the worst, most prevalent disease today and it will, potentially, ruin the native people, according to Chief Jacob Thomas.

Chief Jacob Thomas talked about how alcohol and Christianity helped change the minds of the native people. Many techniques were used in the old days to re-educate them. He talked of the old gentleman who at one time told him, "You know they try and they try to get power and change the native people from their own ways. During the trade days, they killed the animals in order to starve the native people. Now today you have too many animals and the white man does not know what to do with them."

He continued, "The English and French even tried to change the food the native people ate. They would say this is better for you. They took our corn, beans, and squash away from us. They tried to teach us different methods of farming and refused to allow us to hunt anymore. The result was that the people did not grow corn, beans, or squash anymore and did not hunt anymore. This is what the elders would tell me."

Jake talked about going with an elder to the Allegheny River (near Salamanca, New York State) in the forties to a place where the Iroquois once launched their canoes full of furs. He told how they would go downstream to Pennsylvania with their canoes laden with furs and dried meats. They were all young men. In those days they would go downstream for miles to trade, in order to support the elders and their families who lived at home.

In the early days the young men would hunt for pelts. They were very wise back then. They may have looked stupid and seemed like animals to the Europeans, but remember that animals know more than we do.

Jake stretched his hand out in front of me and said, "The elders say that animals have ten days of warning about what is coming. This is the reason they have antlers. They can use them as we use antennae. Even bugs have little antennae for receiving messages. If you look at a deer antler and follow it from the end, it has a pad going right into a single point where it connects to the head. It looks just like the palm of your hand. The points help to tell them what is happening over here and over there. All these points join back into the power of one. That is why the deer and the moose stand still — to receive the vibrations around them. They know much more than we give them credit for. This is why many great leaders wore antlers as part of their headdress.

"In former days, the animals knew the movements of the native peoples; they knew what was in their minds. Even today, you cannot keep your thoughts from animals. Any animal can reveal to you the signs of future happenings if you open yourself up to them. This is also true of birds. Today we ignore this knowledge."

When native people hunted animals, they did so in a way that helped keep a balance. Many people believe that natives lived on venison alone, but that is not true. They changed their diet with each season. In the fall they would go hunting, because there were no more green vegetables; the winter was the time to eat meat and to allow nature to rejuvenate. In June, July, and August, the animal kingdom was restored and native people refrained from hunting. This was true of fishing, too. The elders said that one should not fish until the water becomes cold in the fall. The same thing is true of medicine. Medicine regains its power in the fall. You can see this in animals because in the spring they shed their fur and in the fall they grow more fur for the winter. This is the time that meat is again good to eat. The white man continues to operate outside of the cycles of life. They fish in the summer and hunt year-round.

Chief Jacob Thomas spoke of cycles according to the month as well as the season. "The month of October," he said, "is the time when the meat becomes good again. This month is known by the red leaves on the trees. One should hunt through October and November and in the beginning of December. The new moon in December marks the end of the hunting season. Hunters should hunt bucks only — never the females (does). This allows the deer population to continue to grow for the next season. Today, many hunters simply hunt deer and pay no mind to whether they are male or female.

"Long ago, when the lords of the Confederacy would release the young men to go out hunting, they would be reminded to return on the new moon of December. Upon their return, the people would hold a great Midwinter Ceremony, and the hunters would distribute the meat among the people and offer thanks to the Creator. When fur trading began in North America, the native peoples abandoned the old ways and hunted more than they needed. This led to the loss of harmony with nature and the Creator.

"Today whites and native peoples kill for the wrong reasons: they want the antlers and only the select or tender pieces of meat for eating. There is an imbalance because the animal is not honoured when all parts are not used.

"Native people traditionally had their own special medicine for hunting. They had what was called 'walking medicine,' which was used only at certain times. The medicine would be given to a hunter when he needed more strength to pursue game. Today everything is out of hand with drugs. Drugs are used whether people need them or not, and they are now administered without knowing the spirit or purpose of the individual. Native people knew many of these drugs, but when the non-native people obtained them, they used them for the wrong purpose."

At this point Chief Thomas began to speak about Handsome Lake.

"Handsome Lake experienced this from the time he was young. He experienced alcohol and drugs. The elders say you come to a point in time when the body gives up. This was what happened to Handsome Lake in his life. He was reduced to skin and bones, and for four years he was ministered to by his son-in-law. He prayed every day; he asked the Creator for forgiveness and spoke of changing his attitude; he said he would never touch any evil again in his life. During those years he saw and judged himself; he never blamed anyone else for his state; he never preached at people; he asked only that they take a look at themselves. Handsome Lake would always say you should never judge anyone but yourself; you should never take your troubles to someone else; you should go to the Creator and ask for forgiveness.

"You should never go to the Creator and try to fool him. You should always mean what you say when you talk to the Creator. How many people can do that? We seem to ask for help when we are sick but then forget about our promises to the Creator tomorrow when we are feeling better."

As he cleared his throat and leaned towards the table, I knew Chief Jacob Thomas was about to share a great truth. His gaze remained fixed on me as he spoke. "The Code of

Handsome Lake gave the people of Turtle Island a proph-ecy — a prophecy of what would come to pass. This message is still unfolding. The last change he talked about was to happen somewhere near the year 2000. My grandmother talked about this. She said that three prophets would be sent by the Creator. When Jesus Christ rose from the dead he held up three fingers. No one could understand what that meant. Some thought it meant three weeks, three months, three years, three centuries, before the return of Christ. We are waiting for the third prophet to come.

There is a bridge for all people to cross, a common belief to bring us together. There is only one Creator. He made native people and he also made European people.

Our prophet, Handsome Lake, spoke of the Earth crum-bling. Who can say what that really means? The reason he spoke of crumbling was that there would be so much wrong-doing on the Earth. Will it be an earthquake or will it be people fighting and killing each other because of their beliefs? This will cut off creation. Our way says that the Creator decides how many days you are here. The Creator will be the one to call you. But if someone kills you, they are responsible for cutting off your days. Our days on Earth are not numbered by us. We do not know."

The good sense of his words continues as he begins to speak about the roots of his teachings — the Creator.

"The Creator taught us this to help us think of him each day and each night. You have to be clear about this. People do not think enough about these things. They think they have lots of time to correct their errors; they have a good time now, but what they do not realize is that tomorrow could be their last day. A baby may only cry once and be taken back to the spirit world. There is a reason for this, just as there is a reason when a young person has to leave this world. No one can change what is to be. The Creator makes those decisions for us.

"In our culture everyone has a purpose. No one arrives in this world without a purpose. That is why the Creator gave us a culture. He meant that we should keep that culture going. We have all been given certain gifts and talents. I have a talent to sing and you have a talent to dance or you have a gift of knowledge about ceremonies. You can sing but you cannot speak. The Creator has given us all these gifts and all are part of our culture. He gave someone the talent to be an artist. That artist helps to reinforce a certain belief.

"We are all here for a common purpose. The Creator has given each of us gifts to help one another. We should be generous and do so. If I see you starving, I can give you food; I can also give you clothing if I am better off than you are. Some people have the gift of thinking in a small way; those who have been given the gift to think in a larger way should help those people who have less. This is what it is to be generous with one another and to help one another to get along in peace in this world."

Handsome Lake gave his people a prediction. He said Mother Earth is going to crumble. Chief Jacob Thomas talked about the criticism that was visited upon the native way when the white man arrived. The difference in the native philosophy about the land is becoming much clearer now. Native peoples have always believed in taking care of Mother Earth, but the white man wanted ownership.

There is still, in Chief Jacob Thomas's eyes, misunderstanding about his people's customs and traditions. "When the Europeans arrived and met the native people," he commented, "they called them savages. What most white people do not realize is that they were the savages when they came here. White people always seem to bury their own history and past. Now the young people are going to their elders in white society and asking for stories or traditions. They want to know their origins and history, the beliefs that were held in the past.

"If the native people were savages, then they would have killed every white person that set foot on Turtle Island. Instead, when the whites approached us, we shared the land, because they, too, were people. We did not believe we were better than the whites. Today people often say, 'I'm better than he is.' Today, even my own people are like that. This philosophy seems to have gotten the better of us."

At that moment, Chief Jacob Thomas looked away and paused before he continued his line of thinking. "When the Jews met their prophet, many did not believe. They eventually crucified their own teacher. It was said during the time of Handsome Lake that our own people would turn away and not believe in the message. I think we have almost reached that point now. The predictions of Handsome Lake have all come true. What will people do when the sun no longer shines? There will be many on their hands and knees praying. What will we do when the rain no longer come? There could come a time when there is no water. People always think they can manage, no matter what happens. I tell you, when the thunderers no longer come, people will not manage. That is why, when we come together to give thanks for all things, we give thanks to the Creator for what has been provided. We give thanks to the thunderers, the sun, the moon, the stars, and the air that we breathe.

"I often think about the changes and how far we have come. I look at the trees and see that they have already died at the top. I think about the predictions of Handsome Lake about the trees dying from the top down. I can see how nature is beginning to go against people because of their destructive ways. Now we see worms coming and destroying all the plants and trees. This means something today, but in those days they couldn't imagine the meaning behind these predictions. No one could believe the forest would disappear or the water become polluted. This was true of the native peoples and the Europeans. Now we see what was spoken back then. When I was a child, I used to go out and fish in the creek near my grandfather's house. He lived nearby on the reserve, and I crossed over a wooden bridge to get there. I remember how clear the water was, flowing beneath that bridge. Today in the same place you cannot see the bottom of the creek. The water is muddy, polluted, and weedy. The creek itself is very small compared to what it once was."

Chief Thomas is an elder and his wisdom is great. According to him, "Wisdom is meant to be shared, and society is in great need. Now is the time to listen to our elders. Many non-native people are coming to me these days and they are saying that they are Christian but that what they hear from me is what they are looking for. Many young people are pulling away from the church to seek a clearer vision. This is what we are talking about. It does not matter what colour we are, we need to come together. Mother Earth has suffered so much abuse. People say it may take as many years to heal the wounds of our mother the Earth as it took to inflict them. The Code of Handsome Lake says that if everyone would repent of their ways, the Creator could make all things new again. This means to bring back unity, have a good mind, and treat one another as we would ourselves.

"We need only one belief. Why are we so defiant in the way we think? Why must we believe in many gods? Why do we have so many denominations of belief? The Creator gave us a way that was equal and to be shared. We might do it a little differently in ceremony but we always help one another no matter where we go. If I go to the Cree country, I can join with them, but do you think religious denominations like Catholics and Protestants would do the same? We have forgotten that there is only one Creator. Christian groups have the tendency to state that one belief is better than the other belief. It is the same with cults. What Handsome Lake said about the Confederacy was that the hereditary chief was there to uphold the belief and to make sure that all the people followed it."

For Chief Jacob Thomas, this is a time when we need to care for all people. This results in peace of mind. It eliminates the need to discriminate against people because of colour or creed. It matters not to him if those he meets are native or non-native; he relates to all in the same way, because they are human. He does not wish to be treated any differently than anyone else. He knows that we need to learn to be this way with one another.

He adds, "We can see this strongly in the European belief 'Love they neighbour.' Where I live in Six Nations Territory along the Grand River, near Tuscarora Township and Brant-ford, Ontario, we live next to non-natives, but many discrim-inate against us. This is not practising a good mind. People do not live in agreement. The same is true of native peoples.

They are not of one mind either. They live in separation and fight amongst themselves.

"People need to remember the Longhouse. We need to take a look at the community. We have always shared the teachings. This meant doing things together and getting along with one another. This was the reason behind the Longhouse and the clan system. The Europeans had clan systems but they were not maintained."

Chief Jacob Thomas believes most white people today have lost touch with their inherited culture and that some native peoples are confused about theirs. This confusion came because the Europeans wanted to convert the native people to their way of thinking. The early Jesuits once said, "Think about your soul." What does that mean? Jake says it means that what they preached was for you to watch out for your soul but to forget about your land, and as a result people began to care more about their souls than about the land.

"I have heard the expression 'a melting pot for all native people.' Some whites would like to put all native peoples in one pot. Education and the preaching of Christianity are part of this attempt to make us all the same. Some people are clinging to a mere bubble of their culture. I like to use the analogy of being a bowl of fruit cocktail. All the native people will become fruit cocktail, then no one will be able to tell one from another. We will begin to forget our native identity. That is how it is with native people. Now that we are in that one big melting pot, we have confusion and loss of traditions.

"We must learn about our clan fire when we talk of culture and its significance. The Creator gave us fire right from the beginning of time. The fire was provided to bring warmth to the body and peace and comfort to the soul. Without fire, there will be no culture and no righteousness. Fire means peace, power, and a good mind. It takes a good mind to keep that fire burning. When we burn the sacred native tobacco, the smoke rises to the sky world and to the Creator. This is a sacred connection. Other cultures shared this same connection. This melting pot that people speak of will create a loss of our identity and our connection to the Creator. The melting has already caused us to lose our identity, culture, and spiritual connection with our Creator."

When Jake speaks of fire, he speaks of smoke, air, and water and how they are all interconnected. "First you have fire before you burn tobacco. Tobacco comes from Mother Earth and is connected with your mind. Therefore, when you burn tobacco, you send messages to the Creator with your mind. It must be remembered that it is up to the Creator to answer your messages.

"If there is anything wrong with your health, the medicine man will use a fire, mix his medicine with water, and use tobacco and the smoke that rises to the Creator to bring help. This shows how everything is connected and how air helps to carry the smoke to the sky world. The native peoples still have medicine men, but they are few because of the attitudes and brainwashing of white culture."

Jake continues, "Today, we have become a lazy people and we have lost interest in our medicine. Most native people have been led to believe that it is better to go to a doctor than to a medicine man. This has resulted in a loss of knowledge of our medicine. My grandmother was a medicine person. She taught me many things about medicine and healing. Today, many charge for this knowledge, but this is wrong. Handsome Lake speaks about this in the Code. We cannot charge for what the Creator has given us freely."

Recently Jake was ill and unable to cure himself. He went to a Chinese doctor for help. The doctor said he could give him a prescription, but he said it would not help him. "You might think it will help you," he said. "However, the drug will wear off. Then you will be back to see me for another prescription. This would all be in your mind and not help you at all. In time you could become addicted to the drug. The only way I can help you is to give you acupuncture." So Jake tried that and it worked. The doctor was right in the way he did things. Different peoples have different gifts and knowledge in the area of medicine.

Separation and resentment are very prevalent today. Chief Jacob Thomas sees how people always seem to put the categories "non-native" and "native" at the front of their minds. He hears people speak and say "I'm native" or "I'm non-native." He sees confusion around the word "native." He asks "What do people really mean when they use the word 'native' or 'non-native'?" He feels that this is the land of the Creator and that we are all natives of this Earth. No matter what country you come from, he thinks everyone is a native wherever they are. There are no non-natives. Some people call him an Indian, but he does not see himself as an Indian or as a native. He calls himself "Ongwehónwe," meaning "a real person."

This takes us back to the heavenly world — to the story of Creation when the woman came from the sky-world and rested on the turtle's back and the Creator assigned her to become Mother Earth. Soon she bore a child, and that is where the Creator was born — on this Earth. There is a

Master of Life up there whom we never see, but the Creator was born on Earth. Chief Jacob Thomas wonders about Europeans and their Lord. In his culture you never ever see the real Master of Life. He never appears, but sends prophets. The Creation story of the Iroquoian peoples tells how woman was the first one to walk Mother Earth. This is why they follow the bloodline of the women and live in matriarchal tribes. They are made from the spirit of Mother Earth. That is the reason the body goes back to the Earth when we die and becomes Mother Earth once again. This is why we carry a spirit and a soul. When we die, the soul goes back to the Creator and the spirit to the Mother.

"I don't claim to be a full traditionalist, but I can explain my knowledge as it was explained to me," Chief Jacob Thomas said. "I dress like a white man and sometimes I think like a white man. I speak his language and I drive a car. Without these things, I might be considered traditional. When I was a child, I was a traditionalist. I spoke all the languages of the Iroquois and still do. I did not speak English or wear these clothes or have a car, but this changed when I was sent to school."

He went on to say, "It seems you can only be a traditionalist when a pow-wow comes up and money is offered for competing in dances. People may wear the traditional clothes but inside they may not be traditional. The only reason many wear the clothes is for money."

Language is an important part of Jake's teachings. He feels that you cannot learn your culture or knowledge unless you know the language. If the knowledge disappears, all is lost. According to Jake it was once said by a Canadian political leader (Pierre Trudeau), that if you no longer speak your language and no longer practise your culture, then you have no right to demand aboriginal rights or claim land from the Canadian government, because you are assimilated with the ruling power (First Ministers' Conference 1983). Jake feels that the language you speak is that which makes you what you are.

Returning to Handsome Lake, Chief Jacob Thomas spoke of how the Code reveals what is happening to Mother Earth today. Handsome Lake spoke of pollution, but at the time he may not have understood what pollution really meant. We are the ones who can see what pollution really involves. It was a difficult job for Handsome Lake to speak to the people of things that they might not understand. He needed patience and perseverance, but some people refused to believe and turned on him.

Handsome Lake was unable to use force, so he used judgement. Wherever he went, he was always guarded by an escort. This became a tradition among the Iroquois people, that a preacher would always have a guardian and need not be alone. Whenever the Code is recited today, there is a guardian sitting nearby.

Chief Jacob Thomas expressed his concerns about some who do not follow the Code. "The Warrior Society does not believe in the Code of Handsome Lake. They do not follow the Great Law, and their own self-interest comes before the benefit of all nations." They are reputed to be involved in gambling and smuggling and have been accused of using the Great Law for their own ends instead of living by the Great Law.

The Iroquois Warrior Society first appeared in 1924 when the Superintendent of Indian Affairs and the Royal

Canadian Mounted Police forced the Confederacy at Ohsweken out of their own council house. Then, during the late 1960s, a revival of militancy swept across native territory in North America. The Mohawk were at the forefront of the movement. Over the next few years the Society grew in numbers and held longhouse meetings in such places as Kahnawake in Quebec and Akwesasne in New York State. By the 1980s, as many as a hundred Mohawk men and women were attending Warrior Society meetings at a variety of Mohawk communities.

During this same period of time, the Longhouse was gaining followers on the Akwesasne reserve. The community of Akwesasne became divided between Christians and Long-house followers and perhaps of even more importance, the Akwesasne Longhouse was divided into opposing factions: those who supported the Warrior Society and those who disagreed with it and the way they represented the Great Law. These opponents of the Warrior Society also disagreed with gambling and with taking up arms. The differences between the groups were heightened when the lure of cigarette smuggling, cheap gasoline, and casinos came into the community. Suddenly bus and car loads of non-natives travelled to Akwesasne to gamble and buy cigarettes and gasoline.

By the second half of the 1980s, huge profits were being made from cigarettes and gambling at Akwesasne. The Warrior Society grew in wealth and armed themselves, which meant that they could now take a militant stand against outside interference and from natives who did not believe in their governing philosophy.

On July 11, 1990, the Mohawks of Kanesatake near the

town of Oka stood their ground against an attack from outside authorities who wanted to use their land for a golf course expansion. What was unclear to most people at the time was the issue of land ownership. Although the Mohawks did not hold clear title to the land, in their eyes, the land was still theirs. They had become totally exasperated after a century of failed requests for a land claim settlement. This golf-course expansion was the last straw. What began as a quiet protest turned into a seventy-eight-day stand-off backed by the Warrior Society.

Chief Thomas comments, "There were many people in Canada, the United States, and the world over who never really knew what was going on with the Mohawks at Oka. The Warrior Society was asking for support from everywhere.

"The Warrior Society claimed to be acting in accordance with the Great Law by protecting their people. If they were protecting their people, why did they turn their guns on their own people? At Akwesasne in 1989 two native people were killed during a crossfire attack between pro-gamblers and anti-gamblers, but no one really knows who did it. The Warrior Society members call themselves traditional, but they are warriors. They are very powerful today, and if you question them you could be threatened. I was one of the few people who stood up and said, 'If you want to shoot me go ahead. I have something to die for.' Four years ago the Warrior Society threatened to shoot me if I didn't watch myself. I received this message twice."

Raising his voice, Chief Jacob Thomas said, "I don't have to watch myself. People cannot watch over me. The only one who will watch over me is the Creator. He will see what is right and what is wrong. People were quick to jump on the bandwagon for the native people, but no one really knew what they were getting involved in. They wanted to support the Mohawks, but they did not know who they were really supporting. People did not realize that the Mohawks were divided over taking up arms. The Mohawks will never come together as long as they believe differently about the Warrior Society and gambling. There is much that people really do not know.

"This is what happens when a nation no longer follows its traditional teaching. There is disunity, violence, and warring. But there is still the possibility of change if we can practise a good mind once again."

Chief Jacob Thomas explained the idea of a good mind. "The answers are there if people would only listen. The teachings are there for people to follow to make you a better human being. People are too occupied thinking about so many things that are not relative to the law of life.

"The Creator did not intend people to make war and shed blood. The one thing about bloodshed is that it never ends. Something has to end it. In our teaching the Creator gave us three things. He gave us peace, power, and righteousness. He also gave us appreciation, love, respect, and generosity. This is what you carry in your mind. When you have this type of mind, you will be a good human being and behave according to the Creator's law. You will appreciate having good health. You will carry peace in your mind, and no matter who you meet or where you go, you will always have this in your mind. There is no fear with a good mind. If you have a bad mind, fear is always following you. If people go against a good mind, they will always make fools of themselves."

He feels that generosity is the one thing that will bring about unity and a good mind. Being generous includes showing respect to another person. If I respect another person, it is because I wish to show my good feelings. This became a tradition to us. We respect people for what they have, and if they lose something and you find it, you respect the fact that it must belong to someone. So you give it back the way you found it. How many people live up to that today? He asks. If they find a wallet full of money, they will take the money and throw the wallet away. Everybody should believe in this respect, and honour what others have. Respect also pertains to rape. I could not rape a woman, because I respect her. This is what is meant by having a good mind.

"The same is true of property," Chief Jacob Thomas adds. "If I came to your place and saw a stick across the doorway, it meant you did not have to lock the door. In early days we had no locks, so we put a stick or broom across the door and visitors could just walk in. I have given you permission to come in, but you must respect what is in the house. You cannot take anything.

"Many people today are so narrow-minded and do not know what it means to have a good mind. This is why we are so divided today and lack unity. Our people are educated to be self-sufficient, but this takes away from a good mind. They are looking out for themselves, rather than the nation. Our law is to share everything we have. Everyone wants to be happy, but no one can find this happiness. Happiness is connected to the way of thinking that the Creator has given us. Everyone thinks differently. Some people think more about ways of living better. Some people think less, and it is up to those who think more to help the people that think less and make it easier for them. This allows everyone to feel good and be happy.

"When we talk of our traditions we never hide the truth of our history from our children. We are honest about our faults and share this with our people. But do white people do that?

"We speak the truth to help our people become better human beings. Whites keep real history away from their people. They hide poverty, theft, and murder from others. Instead of learning from the past and changing it, they create repetition by denying historical truths. This is why people have continued the practice of things like war.

"This pattern of killing has moved to the city streets and to the killing of one's own father, mother, sister, brother — and all because of having no respect for one another. White people will not admit to these wrongs in their past, so they can look good in the present. But people do not learn this way. People need to know the truth about their families and nation to gain peace of mind."

Chief Jacob Thomas spoke of how families and nations came together to respect this good mind. Since the beginning of creation, native people have had a family clan system, which was set up so that families could learn how to comfort and support one another during times of need and to help settle matters in their village. The clans represented a way of life in terms of character and respect.

The clan system began long ago when a wise man told the people to follow him and he would show them how to comfort one another and how to settle differences and make decisions about their lives. He took the people down to a river, where they saw a huge tree with a wild grapevine that grew down from the branches and stretched across the river.

The wise man led the way, and as they crossed the river, the vine shifted. Some people were carried to the other side and others were not. Now the people were divided: some were on one side, some were on the other side, of the water. He then advised them to camp where they were for the night and told them that whoever went for water and wood in the morning should remember what they saw.

Early the next morning, those who went to the river saw an eel and a turtle, and those who went into the woods saw a kildeer and a hawk. As they continued, they saw a bear and a deer. The group camped on the other side of the river saw a wolf, a turtle, a heron, and a beaver. The wolf and the deer became the two leading clans of the Iroquois, representing both sides of the river.

Then the wise man said, "Now these things you have seen will be your clans. This river that has divided you, has shown you that the clans of nations on one side of the water will support the clans of nations on the other side. This is the way it shall always be. One nation will support another, and in this way you will reach consensus. All the different clans will become one voice. Everyone will have a voice in each clan. Anytime you have something to discuss, you will come together and reach consensus and support one another in the decision making. When there is a death in a clan, another clan may come forth to console and comfort the other clan members, thus achieving respect in the nation."

Chief Thomas talked of the Mohawk nation and how their clan system has three divisions. They have the Turtle, Wolf, and Bear clans. So when they sit in council to make decisions, all three clans have to reach consensus. When they reach consensus, they become one voice as one nation.

"Everyone is born into a clan," Chief Jacob Thomas continued, "and the clan name is always passed down through the mother's side. My mother was Cayuga and my great-grandmother was Cayuga. This is why I could become a chief, because I fit into the bloodline of the Sandpiper clan. It is up to the clan mother to decide if I am worthy enough to become chief. This chieftainship could be taken away from me at any time if my conduct is not appropriate in the eyes of the clan mother. We have only one chief of that clan. I am the chief of the Sandpiper clan of the Cayuga nation."

Chief Jacob Thomas closed with thoughts on values and culture, saying, "I believe every native person should understand why it is so important to learn their native language. Language was here before any kind of religion was ever practised, and that language reflected a way of life.

"Language consists of the most important set of symbols used by human beings. These symbols extend beyond the physical world for which they stand; they express the culture of the people and offer a way of referring to events gone by and yet to come.

"Native people need to understand that to speak a language is to give voice to the culture."

Our conversation had come to an end, and we were both content. With a warm "thank you" from Jake, our literary journey that had begun on a bright and sunny morning had come to the end of its first phase.

This had been done in honour, respect, peace, and the desire to share.

Bibliography

Culin, Stuart. *Games of the North American Indians*. New York: Dover Publications, 1975.

Parker, A.C. *The Code of Handsome Lake, The Seneca Prophet*. Ohsweken, Ontario: Iroqrafts Ltd., 1990. Originally published 1912.

Wallace, Anthony. *The Death and Rebirth of the Seneca*. New York: Random House, 1972.

York, Geoffrey, and Loreen Pindera. *People of the Pines*. Toronto: Little, Brown Canada, 1992.